What people are saying about Dr. Myles Munroe's books...

God has an exciting purpose, plan, and vision for every one of His children. If you haven't found yours yet, *The Principles and Power of Vision* will help you discover and fulfill your God-ordained destiny. This is truly one of the best books I've ever read on the topic of vision!

Bill McCartney
Founder and President, Promise Keepers

What a great book! Myles Munroe has captured a clear and concise roadmap for discovering the vision for our lives and, more succinctly than anyone else, how to fulfill it.

Dr. Bill Winston
Pastor, Living Word Christian Center
Forest Park, Illinois

The Principles and Power of Vision seeks to inspire men and women to pursue the vision that God has placed in their hearts and is also a practical tool for maximizing one's potential. The book is spiritually and mentally stimulating as it explores the concept that "vision" is powerful and a motivator to human activity, and that it requires the application of basic rules and principles for effective fulfillment.

I congratulate Dr. Munroe on the success of this book, which is indicative of the desire within readers for such material. I have no doubt that Dr. Munroe's desire to impart his insights and concepts to the world through this medium will bear much fruit.

I highly commend this book to individuals in all aspects of leadership—spiritual and secular—and pray that God will bless those who strive to fulfill the vision He has placed in them.

Dame Ivy Dumont
Governor-General
The Commonwealth of the Islands of the Bahamas

After reading your book,...I was challenged to my marrows. I began to see the potential hidden in me which needs to be tapped.

Evangelist Chidiebere
Nigeria

Your book on potential touched my life. It made me realize that I am pregnant with lots of things that I have to bring out. I need to be a young man who is fully committed to God.

Phineas Mahlatsi
South Africa

As one who has been enriched through the teachings and writings of Dr. Myles Munroe, I find the message in *Understanding the Purpose and Power of Men* both significant and challenging.... This is an on-time and end-time book, not just to read, but to be used as a reference in charting our course for a better society and a richer life.

Dr. Bill Winston
Pastor, Living Word Christian Center
Forest Park, Illinois

Understanding the Purpose and Power of Men helps males understand what it means to be a man, husband, and father so they can become change agents towards rebuilding families, communities, and ultimately a nation.

Mr. Jerome Edmondson
President and Founder
Christian Business Network, Inc.
Southfield, Michigan

Your book, *Understanding the Purpose and Power of Men,* is one of the best books I have read. It has brought my relationship with God alive.

Terry Hall
Oregon

I finished reading *Understanding the Purpose and Power of Prayer.* It is an awesome teaching. You will never know how it has touched my spirit and life.

Mary Campbell
Westport, Indiana

THE PRINCIPLES AND

POWER

OF

VISION

THE PRINCIPLES AND

POWER

OF

VISION

KEYS TO ACHIEVING
PERSONAL AND CORPORATE DESTINY

DR. MYLES MUNROE

WHITAKER
HOUSE

THE PRINCIPLES AND POWER OF VISION:
Keys to Achieving Personal and Corporate Destiny

Munroe Global
P.O. Box N9583
Nassau, Bahamas
www.munroeglobal.com
office@munroeglobal.com

ISBN: 978-1-62911-371-5 • eBook ISBN: 978-1-60374-141-5
Printed in the United States of America
© 2003 by Munroe Group of Companies Ltd.

Whitaker House
1030 Hunt Valley Circle
New Kensington, PA 15068
www.whitakerhouse.com

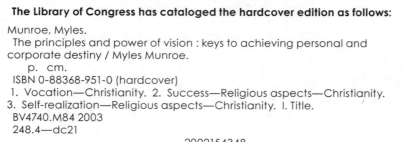

The Library of Congress has cataloged the hardcover edition as follows:
Munroe, Myles.
 The principles and power of vision : keys to achieving personal and corporate destiny / Myles Munroe.
    p. cm.
 ISBN 0-88368-951-0 (hardcover)
 1. Vocation—Christianity. 2. Success—Religious aspects—Christianity.
 3. Self-realization—Religious aspects—Christianity. I. Title.
 BV4740.M84 2003
 248.4—dc21
                              2002154348

9 10 11 12 13 14 ᴡ 26 25 24 23

Dedication

To the visually impaired among us. May the visions of your hearts replace the limitations of your eyes.

To my spiritual father and mentor, Oral Roberts, whose visionary leadership accomplishments inspired my own.

To Richard Pinder III, my faithful friend and partner in vision. Your faith and belief in me and the vision over the years has encouraged me.

To my executive leadership team at BFMI. Thank you for your visionary support.

To the millions of people in the developing Third-World countries who daily aspire to believe in a vision of a better world. I believe, also.

To my beloved wife Ruth, daughter Charissa, and son Chairo. Thanks for believing.

To the Source of all true visions and the Sustainer of all dreams.

Acknowledgments

This work is the result of a lifetime of learning and development from many mentors, teachers, supporters, advisors, pastors, counselors, friends, and family, who invested their time, energy, and interest in my life. For this, I am eternally grateful.

No achievement in life is without the help of many known and unknown individuals who have contributed to our lives. We are all the sum total of what we have learned from others, and we owe any measure of success to the array of input from so many. Here are just a few who made this work possible:

To my wife Ruth, for your unwavering support.

To Lois Puglisi, my talented and excellent editor. Your relentless pursuit of and patience with me during the inception, incubation, development, and delivery of this work was a tremendous source of motivation and encouragement. You're a writer's dream.

To the members and followers of BFMI who allowed me the privilege of sharing and testing the ideas and principles in this book in our relationship over the years. Without you, my vision would have remained just a dream. I am forever grateful.

To the friends and distinguished members of the Board of Trustees of the International Third World Leaders Association, for your example of visionary leadership over the years. You inspired me to believe in mine.

To my friend, Jim Rill, who helped with the early stages of the development of this work and the conceptual development of the cover design. You are a part of my history. Thank you.

Contents

Preface..11

Introduction: Life without Vision 15

PART I: WHAT IS VISION? 20

  1. Vision: The Key to Fulfilling Your Life's Purpose...........21

  2. The Source of Vision...41

  3. Overcoming Obstacles to Vision 63

PART II: TWELVE PRINCIPLES FOR FULFILLING PERSONAL VISION 78

Introduction to Part II..79

  4. PRINCIPLE 1: Be Directed by a Clear Vision......................81

  5. PRINCIPLE 2: Know Your Potential for
                    Fulfilling Vision 91

  6. PRINCIPLE 3: Develop a Concrete Plan for
                    Your Vision 99

  7. PRINCIPLE 4: Possess the Passion of Vision 109

  8. PRINCIPLE 5: Develop the Faith of Vision 119

  9. PRINCIPLE 6: Understand the Process of Vision.............129

 10. PRINCIPLE 7: Set the Priorities of Vision 137

 11. PRINCIPLE 8: Recognize People's Influence
                    on Vision 151

 12. PRINCIPLE 9: Employ the Provision of Vision 165

13. PRINCIPLE 10: Use Persistence in Achieving
                     the Vision 189

14. PRINCIPLE 11: Be Patient in the Fulfillment
                     of Vision 203

15. PRINCIPLE 12: Stay Connected to the Source
                     of Vision 209

PART III: THE POWER OF VISION 214

16. The Generational Nature of Vision 215

17. How to Write Your Personal Vision Plan 217

Taking Action: Action Steps to Bringing Your Vision
into Reality 223

A Word to Third-World Nations 231

About the Author 235

Preface

Vision is the source and hope of life. The greatest gift ever given to mankind is not the gift of sight, but the gift of vision. Sight is a function of the eyes; vision is a function of the heart. "Eyes that look are common, but eyes that see are rare." Nothing noble or noteworthy on earth was ever done without vision. No invention, development, or great feat was ever accomplished without the inspiring power of this mysterious source called vision.

Civilizations were born and developed through the driving power of a visionary leader. The canvas of history is painted with evidence of the creative, tradition-defying force of vision. Social, economic, architectural, medical, scientific, and political achievement and advancements owe their conception and birthing to the power of vision.

Any civilization that is trapped in a time warp of the past, suffocated by the traditions of past experiences and buried in the grave of the glories of past successes, is doomed to die. Vision is the key to unlocking the gates of what was and what is, to propelling us into the land of what could be, and has not yet been. Vision sets you free from the limitations of what the eyes can see and allows you to enter into the liberty of what the heart can feel. It is vision that makes the unseen visible and the unknown possible.

Vision also makes suffering and disappointment bearable. Vision generates hope in the midst of despair and provides endurance in tribulation. Vision inspires the depressed and motivates the discouraged. Without vision, life would be a study in cyclic frustration within a whirlwind of despair. Vision is the foundation of courage and the fuel of persistence.

It was vision that inspired the first biblical civilization established by the great hunter Nimrod. Vision produced the great Egyptian civilization over four thousand years ago and gave rise to the towering pyramids that still amaze us today. Vision inspired the Greeks to produce philosophy and art that still impact the thinking of our world. Vision motivated the great Roman empire to expand its influence and colonize the known world. Vision inspired the explorers who circumvented the globe and ignited the creation and expansion of many of the nations that we know today. Vision transformed the agricultural world into the industrial age. Vision gave birth to the thousands of inventions in the last two centuries that have transformed our lives.

It was the vision of flight that inspired the Wright brothers to invent the airplane. It was the vision of light that possessed Thomas Edison to invent the lightbulb. It was the vision of a desk-sized computer that motivated Stephen Jobs to invent the desktop computer. It was the vision of giving every person access to people-friendly software that inspired Bill Gates to develop and invent the Microsoft global empire. Vision is the energy of progress.

Our world today is in desperate need of vision. Even a casual look at the prevailing conditions in our twenty-first century world is enough to produce fear, hopelessness, uncertainty, insecurity, emotional and social trauma, depression, disillusionment, discouragement, and despair. The threat of economic collapse, social disintegration, moral decay, religious conflict, political instability, global health epidemics, ethnic cleansing, and the clash of civilizations demands leadership that can see beyond the now into a preferred future, that has the skill to transfer that vision into reality, and that has the courage to inspire us to go there.

The wise king of Israel, Solomon, stated in his book of Proverbs, *"Where there is no vision, the people perish"* (Proverbs 29:18

KJV). These words have been quoted and repeated by millions of people over the years because they capture the significant role vision has in our individual, corporate, and national lives. The full essence of his statement implies that where there is no revelation of the future, people throw off self-control, personal discipline, and restraint. Simply put, vision is the source of personal and corporate discipline.

There are many who have no vision for their lives and wonder how to obtain one. There are others who have a vision, but are stuck in the mud of confusion not knowing what to do next. Then there are those who had a vision but have abandoned it because of discouragement, disillusionment, some measure of failure, or frustration. If you are in one of these categories, *The Principles and Power of Vision* is designed to help you understand the nature of vision, define vision, capture or recapture a personal vision, simplify your vision, and document your vision.

I also hope to help you understand the principles of vision and to provide the practical tools and skills necessary to bring your vision into reality. You were born to achieve something significant, and you were destined to make a difference in your generation. Your life is not a divine experiment, but a project of Providence to fulfill a purpose that your generation needs. This personal purpose is the source of your vision and gives meaning to your life. I therefore encourage you to believe in your daydreams and to reconnect with your passion; your vision awaits your action. Your future is not ahead of you—it lies within you. See beyond your eyes and live for the unseen. Your vision determines your destiny.

Introduction:
Life without Vision

In the mid-twentieth century, in Bangkok, Thailand, the government wanted to build a large highway through a village. Yet in the path of the planned road was a Buddhist monastery with a little chapel, so they had to relocate the monastery—including a heavy, eleven-foot clay statue of Buddha—to another place. Using a crane, the government workers moved the monastery in sections. When the workers transported the statue of Buddha to the new location and began to lower it into place, however, the clay on the statue started to crumble and fall off. The people were afraid because this was a precious religious symbol to them, and they didn't want it to be destroyed. Yet the more the workers tried to place the statue, the more it fell apart until, eventually, all the clay was falling off. Suddenly, the workers stared in amazement because, as the clay fell away, something unexpected was revealed: The statue was pure gold underneath. Before the statue was moved, people thought it was worth about fifty thousand dollars. Today, that golden Buddha is worth millions and, because of the story behind it, is visited by hundreds of thousands of people every year.

This story illustrates that what we can see is not necessarily what really is. I believe that many of us are living as clay vessels when, in reality, we are pure gold inside. Our lives do not reflect who we truly are or what we can be. I travel around the world speaking to various groups, and I meet people on every continent who have no sense of personal purpose. I see them struggling with aimless or misdirected lives.

15

A lack of purpose and unfulfilled potential is epidemic in our world. Yet just as the gold statue was hidden inside the clay one, the "gold" inside each of us is waiting to be revealed. This gold is the dreams we have—or once had—for our lives that are not yet reality, the gifts and talents that we have not yet developed, the purpose for our lives that is not yet fulfilled, the "something" we've always wanted to be or do but for some reason have not been able to accomplish.

No matter who you are or what country you live in, you have a personal purpose, for every human being is born with one. God created each person with a unique vision. He has tremendous plans for you that no one else can accomplish. The tragic thing is that many people live their whole lives without ever recognizing their visions.

How do you remove the clay and uncover the gold within you? Your dreams, talents, and desires can be refined in a process of discovering and fulfilling your life's vision so that the pure gold of your unique and personal gifts to this world can shine forth.

Helping you capture and fulfill your vision is the purpose of this book. My own life's vision is the transformation of followers into leaders and the maximization of individual potential, and I'm excited about the potential within you right now. Every person is a leader in his or her own vision, because that person is the only one who can imagine, nurture, and fulfill it. What is your vision? What have you always wanted to do? What is your heart's desire? What is your dream? When you can begin to see your vision clearly, you will be able to fulfill your life's purpose.

What does it mean to capture the vision for your life? Ted Engstrom, the former president of World Vision, told a story that went something like this: A little girl was on a cruise ship, and she and her father were standing on the deck. It was a beautiful clear day, and the air was crisp and fresh. The little girl, standing on tiptoe, said to her father, "I can't see anything." The father picked her up and put her on his shoulders, so that she was higher than everyone else on the deck and was able to see everything around her. "Daddy!" she exclaimed. "I can see farther than my eyes can look!"

That little girl's statement captures the essence of vision: the ability to see farther than your physical eyes can look—to see not just what is, but also what can be and to make it a reality. Vision is a conception that is inspired by God in the heart of a human. The greatest gift God ever gave humanity is not sight, but vision. Sight is a function of the eyes, but vision is a function of the heart. You can have sight but no vision. Throughout history, progress has been made only by people who have "seen" things that were not yet here. Vision is seeing the future before it comes into being. It is a mental picture of your destiny. God gave humanity the gift of vision so we would not have to live only by what we see. The words *vision* and *revelation* are sometimes used interchangeably. To reveal means to unveil. Something that is unveiled was there all along but could not be seen externally.

Consider this analogy: The destiny of an acorn is a tree. By faith, you can see the tree within the seed. You have a vision of it in your mind's eye because you know the potential in the seed. The same thing is true for you and me. God has given us birth for a purpose, and as far as God is concerned, that purpose is already finished because He has placed within us the potential for fulfilling it. We can see that purpose through faith. To paraphrase the Bible, faith is the substance of things you hope to accomplish, the evidence of things you can see even when others cannot. Only by seeing what is not yet here can you bring something new, creative, and exciting into existence.

For true visionaries, the imaginary world of their visions is more real to them than the concrete reality around them. In fact, a visionary's vision is his reality. There is a story about when Disney World had just opened and had only one ride. Walt Disney was sitting on a bench on the grounds, seeming to just stare into space. One of his workers, who was manicuring the grass, came past him and said, "How are you, sir?" Without looking at the man, he said, "Fine," and kept on staring. So the man said, "Mr. Disney, what are you doing?" "I'm looking at my mountain," he answered. "I see the mountain right there." Walt told his architects about this mountain. As he talked, they wrote down what he said, and then they drew up the plans. Walt died before Space Mountain was built, so he never saw it constructed. When Space Mountain was dedicated, the governor and the mayor were present, and Walt's widow was also there. One of the young men stood up to introduce her, and said, "It's a pity that Mr. Walt Disney is not here today to see this mountain, but we're glad his wife is here." Mrs. Disney walked up to the podium, looked at the crowd, and said, in effect, "I must correct this young man. Walt already saw the mountain. It is you who are just now seeing it."

The most powerful force in life is the force of vision. A young man did a college paper in his economics class on his vision for overnight mail. The professor took a red pen, gave him a "C," and wrote, "Do not dream of things that cannot happen." The young man left school and started Federal Express. I wonder where the professor is today. Your vision determines your destiny. When you can see what is possible and believe that it can come to pass, it makes you capable of doing the impossible.

At age thirteen, I wrote down my vision for my life. I carried it with me all through junior high and high school. Much of what I'm doing right now was on paper when I was a young teenager. Vision makes you persistent. Once you know what you really want and can "see" it, then, no matter what comes against you, you never give up. Persistence in fulfilling one's life purpose comes from vision. As long as a person can hold on to his vision, then there is always a chance for him to move out of his present circumstances and toward the fulfillment of his purpose.

I believe with all my heart that when you have no vision, you will simply relive the past with its disappointments and failures. Therefore, vision is the key to your future. Think about what happens to some football teams that are losing the game at halftime. The players go to the locker room and meet with the coach. The coach changes certain game strategies and gives them a pep talk, telling them what they can accomplish. When they come back out, their whole attitude and perspective seems to have changed, and they win the game.

No matter where you are in life, and regardless of how old or young you are, it can be "halftime" for you. You can reassess your life's strategies and focus on fulfilling your purpose. This book will help you to make the necessary adjustments in your life so you can know how to plan for the future and stop making the same mistakes and decisions that have hindered you in the past. It will answer crucial questions, such as these:

- How can I know what my vision is?
- What do I do if I have multiple interests?
- What are some strategies for overcoming hindrances to my vision?
- How can I set the right priorities for my life?
- What should I do when others criticize my dream?
- How can I make my vision a concrete reality?

By the time you finish this book, you will be able to say, "I can see farther than my eyes can look!" You will be able to see not just what is, but also what can be, so that you can fulfill your personal vision.

—Myles Munroe

Part I

What Is Vision?

Chapter One

Vision: The Key to Fulfilling Your Life's Purpose

GOD HAS PLACED WITHIN EACH PERSON A VISION THAT IS
DESIGNED TO GIVE PURPOSE AND MEANING TO LIFE.

Years ago, during the Christmas season, my wife and I took our children to a large toy store. At the time, my son Chairo was about four years old, and his eyes lit up when he spotted a rocking horse. He climbed on, held tightly to the ears of the horse, and began to rock back and forth. After a few minutes, I tried to get him off, but he became angry. When we were about ready to leave, he was still having a wonderful time on that rocking horse, so we let him continue while we walked through the store one last time and told our daughter it was time to go. When we came back, Chairo was rocking even faster. By then, he had been going for about half an hour, and he was soaking wet with sweat. As I watched him, I felt as if God was saying to me, "That's how most people live. They're working hard, sweating hard, but they're making no real progress in life. They're not going anywhere."

Our world is filled with people who are busy but not ultimately effective or satisfied. They are doing much, expending time and energy, but getting little of value accomplished. Consequently, they spend their lives toiling away but never making any headway.

Where Are You Going in Life?

Consider these statistics of American employees:*

Nearly 50 percent of all U.S. workers feel overwhelmed by a growing number of job tasks and longer working hours.

—Families and Work Institute, 2001

Eighty-eight percent of employees say they have a hard time juggling work and life.

—Aon Consulting, 2000

Only 48 percent of workers aged 35–44 are satisfied with their jobs, down from nearly 61 percent in 1995. Older workers, aged 55–64, also express a low level of satisfaction. Only about 48 percent say they are satisfied.

—Conference Board, 2002

In all income areas, satisfaction levels have fallen since 1995.

—Conference Board, 2002

These statistics show that a number of people in the United States are struggling with job and life satisfaction issues. It's disheartening to work hard and not receive satisfaction and fulfillment from your work. What about your own life? What are you using your precious energy on? What are you accomplishing? Do you get up every day with a sense of anticipation and meaning because you know you're doing what you were born to do? Do you feel that your work is a match for your abilities and personality? Or are you pouring your life into your job without feeling fulfilled or having much to show for it? Have you been spending your life helping to make someone else rich while you are left with little or nothing? Have you secretly thought you were meant to do something significant in life, but you don't know what it is?

One of the dilemmas of contemporary society seems to be a lack of meaningfulness and purpose in everyday life. Some people are acutely aware that they aren't fulfilling their potential. They

* Source: <http://www.fishervista.com/statistics.htm> (31 October 2002)

dread Mondays and live for the weekends because they hate their work. Their whole lives seem centered around the only two days they are free from the trapped feeling they experience at work. They long to pursue their own interests and talents. In *Waiting for the Weekend*, author Witold Rybczynski wrote,

> For many people weekend free time has become not a chance to escape work but a chance to create work that is more meaningful—to work at recreation—in order to realize the personal satisfactions that the workplace no longer offers.*

Other people are fairly content with their lives, but they have a vague sense that there should be more significance to life than they are experiencing. Still others live on a surface level, pursuing a series of emotional highs that leave them empty and constantly searching for the next thrill that might satisfy them. Neither of these groups of people realizes that hidden within them is the key to living a more fulfilling life than they ever imagined.

Do you know why you exist?

Whether they are satisfied or dissatisfied with their lives, the eventual goal of most people is retirement. Yet were we born just to go through certain life rituals—find a job, get married, buy a house, raise children, change jobs or careers, retire—and then die? Or is there more to life?

No Reason for Living

If you ask people, "Why do you exist?" most cannot tell you. They can't explain their purpose in the world. They have no vision for their lives.

Do you have a sense of personal purpose? Do you know why you were born? Does your purpose give you a passion for

---

* Witold Rybczynski, "Waiting for the Weekend," *The Atlantic Monthly,* August 1991. <http://theatlantic.com/issues/91aug/rybczynski-p2.htm> (31 October 2002)

living? You may ask me, "Do I really need to have a reason for my existence?" My answer is, Absolutely! Life is intended to have meaning; you were not born just for the fun of it. If all you have to look forward to after working for years for other people is a gold watch and a pension, then your life is a tragedy in the making. You can know why you exist, and you can experience a remarkable life in light of that knowledge. Life doesn't have to be an aimless, repetitive exercise, because you were not designed to simply ride a rocking horse. You were meant to be going somewhere, to be headed toward a destination.

Living without a Dream

When I speak to groups of people about vision, whether it's in the context of business, government, or the church, I always emphasize the following truth because I believe it is crucial for each one of us to understand: The poorest person in the world is a person without a dream.

Maybe you've never known what you wanted to do with your life. Or maybe you had a dream once but lost sight of it through discouraging circumstances or the busyness of day-to-day living. No matter how much money you may have, if you don't have a clear vision for your life, you are truly poor. It has been said that if you don't know where you're going, any road will take you there. What's worse, you won't even know when you have arrived. Unless you have a definite idea of where you want to go, the chances that you will get there are remote.

The problem is that most people have no vision beyond their current circumstances. Without a vision of the future, life loses its meaning. An absence of meaning then leads to a lack of hope. Whenever people are hopeless about their life situations, they can become resentful of their jobs or families. They feel as if they are wasting their lives, and they start living with a vague but constant internal longing for something more. They may even stop participating in life in any significant way. No matter how much money a person may have, anyone who lives like this is poor. A visionless life is a poverty-stricken existence.

Yet if you can see beyond your present circumstances, if you can have hope for the future, you have true riches, no matter how much money you have in your bank account. That is why the Bible encourages us with these words: "'I know the plans I have for you,' declares the LORD, 'plans to prosper you and not to harm you, plans to give you hope and a future'" (Jeremiah 29:11). It doesn't matter what you currently have or don't have, as long as you can see what you could have. This vision is the key to life because where there's a dream, there's hope, and where there's hope, there's faith—and faith is the substance, or fulfillment, of what you are hoping for. (See Hebrews 11:1.)

The poorest person in the world is a person without a dream.

Living with Unfulfilled Dreams

Having a vision, or a dream, is inherent in being human. What is your dream? What do you imagine yourself doing? What do you want to accomplish? Are you doing what you really want to do with your life?

Maybe you once had ideas of what you wanted to be and do, and you still have those ideas. Do you see yourself becoming a lawyer and starting your own firm? Do you dream of owning a successful boutique where people are waiting in line to buy the fashions you designed? Do you think about owning a day-care center that has a first-class curriculum and services two hundred children? Do you want to write a novel? Do you imagine yourself owning a prosperous business and being able to give more money to your church? Do you dream about going back to school and doing something with your education and academic abilities?

By the end of the work week, many of us are very tired. The question is, After exhausting ourselves, are we any closer to where we wanted to go? People have all kinds of ideas in their minds, but they rarely act on them. This is the pattern that often occurs: Five or ten years will go by, and they still haven't done anything to help realize their dreams. Twenty years will pass, yet they haven't become what they really wanted to be or accomplished what they wanted to build or create.

While the poorest person in the world is a person without a dream, **the most *frustrated* person in the world is someone who has a dream but doesn't know how to bring it to pass**. This is the person whose dream has become a nightmare of unfulfilled expectations. When people feel that they are just wandering through life and wasting their potential, their despair can spill over into other areas of their lives, including their relationships, causing additional heartache. These people come to the end of their lives drained, rather than completed, because there's no relationship between their jobs and their visions; there's no relationship between their present circumstances and their dreams.

It's depressing and frustrating to have an idea for years that you haven't yet seen come to pass. Are you weary of having high expectations that never work out? Maybe by now you have so many unfulfilled dreams that it hurts too much to dream anymore. Perhaps you started to pursue your vision, but you got sidetracked or something went wrong, and you abandoned it— there wasn't enough money, it was too time-consuming, people were working against you, your day job became too demanding, or your family said it would never succeed. Since continuing to pursue your dream was so difficult, you backed off, saying, "Forget it! I'm not going to try to be what I really want to be. I'm going to get a 'regular' job with a secure salary and settle down. I'm going to live as a normal person with normal friends in a normal house with a normal paycheck and be buried in a normal grave."

Born to Be Distinct

You will never be satisfied living that way because you were not created to be "normal." You were designed by God not to blend in, but to stand out. Think of the thousands of kinds of flowers in the world. They are all flowers, but each one is unique in its species. Think of a forest. At first glance, the trees all seem to blend together. When you get closer, however, you see that the shape of each tree is unique. Every type of tree has leaves with a distinct design. Why? Uniqueness is part of God's creation.

Individual design is as true of humanity as it is of nature. God doesn't want any one person to get lost in the midst of everyone else. There are over six billion people on the planet—and not one of them has your fingerprints. We can become complacent about this astonishing truth, yet it is something we must continually remind ourselves of since it is easy to feel lost in the crowd. Some people may consider you to be "just another person," but they are wrong. Don't ever allow anyone to cause you to think of yourself as ordinary. If anyone makes you feel less than you are, just look in the mirror and say, "You original thing, you." You are one of a kind, irreplaceable, original. There is no one else like you on the earth. God made you that way because He wanted you to be perpetually rare.

God has given you a unique vision.

In economics, the value of something is determined by how rare it is. For example, real pearls are costly because they are found only in a small number of mollusks, and they must be searched for. When you buy a real diamond, it is expensive because no two diamonds in the world are alike. Gold is costly because it is difficult to find. It is the same way with oil; it does not (usually) just spring up in your backyard. You generally have to dig deep to find it.

Similarly, God wanted you to be perpetually valuable, so He made you permanently rare. He created you as one of a kind. If you go to a sale at a discount store, you'll notice that many of the dresses, sports coats, or ties on the racks are just alike. You'll see twenty items of clothing with the same pattern and color. They're inexpensive because they were mass produced. If you want an original dress, however, you have to go to a designer.

You are not like mass-produced clothing; God has not placed you on a sale rack. You are Designer-made.

Born with a Unique Vision

God not only created each person on earth with a distinct design, but He also placed in everyone a unique vision. No person can give you this vision. It is only God-given. You can go to as many seminars as possible and receive all kinds of wonderful instruction, but no one except God can give you the idea you were born to fulfill.

The poor man, the rich man, the black man, the white man—every person has a dream in his heart. Your vision may already be clear to you, or it may still be buried somewhere deep in your heart, waiting to be discovered. Fulfilling this dream is what gives purpose and meaning to life. In other words, the very substance of life is for you to find God's purpose and fulfill it. Until you do that, you are not really living.

God has a dream and a vision for you that's supposed to carry you right out into eternity because that's what is pulling it. When you die, you're meant to leave this earth not on a pension but on a purpose. You need to make sure you can say at the end of your life, as Jesus did, *"It is finished"* (John 19:30) and not just, "I am retired," for your dream is much bigger than mere retirement.

Jesus said, *"For this reason I was born, and for this I came into the world, to testify to the truth"* (John 18:37). You must have a clear reason for your life, as Jesus did. I know what mine is. I was born to raise up leaders and to train them so they can impact their entire nations for generations to come. That is my reason for living. I was born to inspire and draw out the hidden leader in every human being I meet. When you are around me, suddenly you are going to feel good about yourself. If you stay around me long enough, you'll start being your true self. Why? I was born for that. I was wired for that. What has God wired you for?

Born to Be Known for Something

Every human being was created to accomplish something specific that *no one else can accomplish*. It is crucial for you to understand this truth: You were designed to be known for something special. You are meant to do something that will make you unforgettable. You were born to do something that the world will not be able to ignore.

The Bible is a great Book for recording the stories of people who did little things that the world can't forget. One example is Rahab, the prostitute, who risked her life for people she didn't even know. She was born to hide Joshua's spies so that the Israelites could defeat Jericho. (See Joshua 2, 6.) Everyone who reads the Old Testament knows about her act of courage.

What has God wired you for?

In the New Testament, there is the story of the woman who took an alabaster jar of perfume and anointed Jesus' head with it. This woman was taking a chance by violating the accepted social code of the day and interrupting a group of men who had gathered for a meal. Yet she decided to pour out her life in gratitude to Jesus, no matter what the consequences. Some of those present severely criticized her because she had "wasted" costly perfume on Jesus when it could have been sold for charitable purposes. Yet Jesus said to them, *"Leave her alone....I tell you the truth, wherever the gospel is preached throughout the world, what she has done will also be told, in memory of her"* (Mark 14:6, 9). No matter how small the act may be, if you put your whole life into it, it won't be forgotten.

A Vision for Your Life

It is a deeply distressing fact that, while we all have been given unique visions, too many of us bury our dreams in a lesser existence, making ourselves a graveyard of God's precious treasure.

Perhaps you are eighteen years old. What have you done so far? Have you spent so much time trying to please your friends that you don't know who you are or what your life is about? If so, you aren't doing yourself any favors. You aren't fulfilling your purpose. You may say you are just reacting to "peer pressure." In reality, you are allowing others to rule your life.

Maybe you are forty years old. What have you done so far that the world can't forget? How long will you drift along without working toward your dream? Procrastination can become a full-time occupation. Some people are experts at it. They know how to avoid the real issues of life with precision. They know how to do nothing all day, or they know how to do everything except what is really important. It's depressing to be around people who are just existing, but it's exciting to be around people who know that they are doing what they were born to do.

Too many of us bury our dreams in a lesser existence, making ourselves a graveyard of God's precious treasure.

Many people spend a lifetime wandering away from who God made them to be because they have never recognized who they are in the first place. For example, perhaps you have been a secretary for twenty years. You are at the same level as when you started, even though you dream of being an administrator. You should move from being a secretary to an executive secretary, from an executive secretary to an administrative assistant, and from an administrative assistant to an administrator. People don't fulfill their visions because they have no sense of destiny. They say, "Well, I have a job. I just want to keep it." Merely holding on to a job is like treading water. Every job should put you on a track toward a goal that is bigger than the present one so that you can fulfill your vision.

We need to be like the apostles, who were known for their acts, not their talk. The biblical book about them is called The Acts of the Apostles because they were doers. They had a destination, and they were busily working toward it. They weren't on a rocking horse. Instead, they were changing systems. They were affecting government. They were transforming the world. Nations were afraid of them, and towns became nervous when they showed up because they were said to have *"turned the world upside down"* (Acts 17:6 NKJV). How do people feel when you show up? Do they say, "Oh, here she comes again. She probably has another new idea"? Change will always upset people who are content to be stagnant, but that shouldn't stop you. You should be known for your vision.

What Your Vision Will Give You

It has been said that there are three kinds of people in the world: First, there are those who never seem to be aware that things are happening around them. Second, there are those who ask, "What just happened?" Third, there are those who *make* things happen.

I have observed firsthand the truth of this statement, paraphrased from John Stuart Mill: One person with vision is greater than the passive force of ninety-nine people who are merely interested in doing or becoming something. Most people have an interest in their destinies, but they have no passion or drive to fulfill them. They don't really believe the dreams God has put in their hearts. If they do believe them, they don't do the things that will take them in the direction of fulfilling them. Yet that is what separates the people who make an impact in the world and those who just exist on the planet.

Have you discovered what your vision is? Finding something you can put your whole self into will fill your life with new hope and purpose. It will give you a reason for living. My purpose has become my passion. It wakes me up in the morning, and it keeps me going when I'm tired. It is an antidote to depression. It causes me to have joy in the midst of great opposition because I know that what God has given me to accomplish cannot be stopped by anyone.

When you discover your vision, it will give you energy and passion. Ecclesiastes 9:10 says, *"Whatever your hand finds to do, do it with all your might."* The vision in your heart is the spark

31

that will enable you to pursue your dream because, unless you do so with all your enthusiasm and strength, it will not happen. I believe this Scripture expresses a truth that most people miss: You accomplish only what you fight for. Again, if you are merely interested in your dream, it will never come to pass. However, if you are willing to put all your energy into it, then nobody can stop it from succeeding.

I believe this Scripture also implies that if you set your hands to do something, there will inevitably be resistance, opposition, and difficulties; therefore, you have to apply pressure in order to fulfill your dream. You must put your whole might behind it. Hard work and diligence are essential ingredients to success, but they require an internal motivation. That internal motivation is vision.

Your purpose will become your passion.

Vision is the primary motivator of human action, and, therefore, everything we do should be because of the vision God has placed in our hearts. Vision influences the way you conduct your entire life, such as what you spend your time and money on and what your priorities are. Without vision, you have no values to guide your living. Life has no sense of direction. Activity has no meaning. Time has no purpose. Resources have no application.

Vision is the juice of life. It is the prerequisite for passion and the source of persistence. When you have vision, you know how to stay in the race and complete it.

Your Gift Will Make a Way for You

How is the fulfillment of vision meant to work in practical terms? Proverbs 18:16 is a powerful statement that reveals the answer: *"A man's gift makes room for him"* (NKJV). You were designed to be known for your gift. God has put a gift or talent into every person that the world will make room for. It is this gift that will enable you to fulfill your vision. It will make a way for you in life. It is in exercising this gift that you will find real fulfillment, purpose, and contentment in your work.

It is interesting to note that the Bible does not say that a man's *education* makes room for him, but that his gift does. Somehow we have swallowed the idea that education is the key to success. Our families and society have reinforced this idea, but we will have to change our perspective if we are to be truly successful. Education is not the key to success. Don't misunderstand me. I believe in education. I'll talk more about the importance of education shortly. However, if education were the key to success, then everyone who has a Ph.D. should be financially secure and happy.

If you are intelligent but are not exercising your gift, you're probably going to be poor. If you're educated but have not developed your talent, you're likely to be depressed, frustrated, and tired; you will hate going to work on Monday mornings. There are those who have degrees in finance who have a hard time making ends meet. Doesn't it make you nervous when people who don't have any money try to tell you how to make a million dollars?

Education, in itself, doesn't guarantee anything; it is your gift that is the key to your success. The second part of Proverbs 18:16 says, *"A man's gift...brings him before great men"* (NKJV). You don't realize that the gift you're sitting on is loaded. The world won't move over for you just because you're smart. Whenever you exercise your gift, however, the world will not only make room for you, but it will also pay you for it. Anyone—yourself included—who discovers his or her gift and develops it will become a commodity. If you're a young person in high school or college who is planning your career, don't do what people say will make you wealthy. Do what you were born to do, because that is where you will make your money. No matter how big the world is, there's a place for you in it when you discover and manifest your gift.

Michelangelo poured his life into his art. That's why we still remember him five hundred years after he lived. Beethoven and

Bach put themselves wholly into their work, and their music lives forever. Alexander Graham Bell believed that sound could be converted into electrical impulses and transmitted by wire. No one remembers all the people who thought Bell was crazy; we remember only the man who had vision enough to create the telephone. Thomas Edison reportedly would spend eight or nine days straight locked up in a room working on his experiments. He didn't just happen to make a mistake and create a lightbulb; he had a dream. Although it took him a long time, he believed that we could harness energy and that it could produce light. Because he believed it, he stayed with it until he saw the fulfillment of his vision. That's what makes him unforgettable.

Anyone who develops his gift will become a commodity.

If you do things in a halfway manner, you will probably always be able to find some sort of job, yet you are going to be simply a mediocre employee. It is when you decide that you're going to find something that is truly yours that you will find your gift, fulfill your vision, and be remembered by others.

Stirring Up Your Gift

While the gift is in us, we have the responsibility to stir it up. The apostle Paul wrote to Timothy, *"For this reason I remind you to fan into flame the gift of God, which is in you"* (2 Timothy 1:6). In the *New King James Version*, the verse is translated, *"Stir up the gift of God."* The gift is not something we learn. It is something God gave us. It is something we need to discover and then stir up. No one else can activate your gift for you. You have to do it yourself.

You stir up your gift by developing, refining, enhancing, and using it. That's where education comes in. Education can't give you your gift, but it can help you develop it so that it can be used to the maximum. Proverbs 17:8 says, *"A gift is as a precious stone in the eyes of him that hath it: whithersoever it turneth, it prosper-eth"* (KJV). In other words, a gift is like a precious stone to the one who has it, and whenever he stirs it up, it turns into prosperity. If you use your gift, it will prosper you. Many people are working for money. That's an inferior reason to work. We must work for the vision within us.

Moreover, you are not to mimic the gifts of others. You are to stir up your own gift. Unfortunately, many people are jealous of other people's gifts. Let me encourage you not to waste your time on jealousy. Jealousy is a gift robber. It is an energy drain that will always take away the passion of life from you. You should be so busy stirring up your gift that you don't have time to be jealous of anyone else or to feel sorry for yourself.

I once read an article about Louis Armstrong, the jazz artist, who reportedly applied to go to music school when he was a young man. At his audition, he was given scales to sing, but he could sing only the first two notes properly, and he was told he didn't have what it takes to be a musician. The story said that he cried at first because he had been rejected from the music program, but that he told his friends afterward, "I know there's music in me, and they can't keep it out." He eventually became one of the most successful and beloved jazz musicians. He sold more records and made more money than scores of others who were more talented at singing. Now he is forever etched in the history of music.

What made the difference? Louis Armstrong put his life into the gift he knew he had, and this gift made room for him. He was an original, and he knew it. He wasn't about to waste time feeling sorry for himself. Instead, he put his energies into developing the musical gift within him.

Although we are all born as originals, most of us become imitators. I used to think about becoming like everyone else and joining the rat race. Yet I soon realized that if all the rats are in a race, and you win, you simply become the Big Rat. I recommend that you get out of the rat race, stop competing with the community, stop being in a contest with society, stop trying to keep up with the Joneses, stop trying to please everybody, and decide, "I'm not going to be a rat. I'm going to find my own niche. I'm going to make room for myself in the world by using my gift."

Perhaps you are fifty-eight, sixty-five, seventy years old. You're looking back over the last fifty years and asking, "What have I done with my life? What have I contributed to the human race? What have I really left for the next generation to know that I was here? I have left no footprint in the sands of history." Do you wish you had had a better understanding of vision when you were younger? Are you thinking, "I'm too old now. I don't have the energy or time to stir up a gift"?

If you believe you're too old to use your gift, you're believing a lie.

I am deeply sorry that many people in the world have worked very hard all their lives and accomplished little. Yet if you believe you're too old to use your gift, you're believing a lie. We read in the Bible that God went to people who were already past retirement age, and He recharged them. They have become noteworthy in history because they started over when others (even they themselves) thought their lives were almost over. (See the stories of Abraham and Sarah in Genesis 18:11–15; 21:1–8, and Elizabeth and Zechariah in Luke 1.) Your gift will give you your youth back. Your gift will give you energy and strength. You'll be healthier. You'll stop talking about dying and start talking about living.

Realizing Your Vision

If you have a dream, or if you want to discover your vision, remember this: *God loves dreamers.* He gives visions, and He is attracted to people who love to dream big. Don't forget that you are unique, special, and irreplaceable. You are not meant to be like anyone else. When you decide to be part of the norm, your destiny is shortchanged. God wants you to stir up the gift He has given you and to develop it to the fullest.

What is the difference between the dreamer who realizes his dream and the dreamer whose dream becomes a nightmare of unfulfilled hopes? The dreamer who succeeds is someone who has a clear vision and acts on it. As long as a person can hold on to his vision, then there is always a chance for him to move out of his present circumstances and toward the fulfillment of his purpose.

If you feel trapped, underemployed, or underutilized in your job; if you own your own business and want it to grow; if you want to know how to pursue your goals in life; if you are the leader of an organization or group; if your children are grown or in school now, and you are considering reviving old interests; or wherever you are in life right now, *The Principles and Power of Vision* will enable you to—

- understand vision and why it is essential to your sucess.
- discover and live out your purpose in life.
- identify your vision's goals and stay on course.
- overcome obstacles to your vision.
- learn the key principles necessary for fulfilling your life's dream.
- develop a specific plan for achieving your vision.
- live the life you were always meant to live.

My desire is that you will be inspired, motivated, and challenged to get back in the race toward your dream, to get back the passion for fulfilling your goal. I want you to achieve your greatest in God's purpose for your life. I want you to get off the rocking horse and find a living stallion—your life's vision.

To do this, you need to understand and practice principles that transcend current trends and even conventional wisdom. Your success will not depend on the state of the economy, what careers are currently in demand, or what the job market is like. You will not be hindered by your initial lack of resources or by what people think you can or cannot do. Instead, the time-tested principles of this book will enable you to fulfill your vision no matter who you are or what your background is.

You are the sum total of the choices and decisions you make every day. You can choose to stay where you are right now, or you can choose to move forward in life by pursuing your dream. I want to challenge you to stop making excuses for why you can't accomplish what you were born to do. Take your life out of neutral. God has given you the power and the responsibility to achieve your life's vision.

Most people do things because they have to. Wouldn't you like to do things because you have *decided* to, based on your purpose? You must choose to be on the offensive rather than the defensive. I hope you will decide you have had enough of being "normal" and that you will declare your distinction. Remember, you were created to stand out, not to blend in. You were designed not only to be special and unique, but also to specialize. You were created to accomplish something that no one else can accomplish.

Never expect anything less than the highest thing you can go after. Don't let people tell you, "You shouldn't have high expectations." Always expect more than what you have, more than what you are currently doing. Dream big. Somewhere inside you there is always the ability to dream. No matter how challenging it gets, don't give up, because *your vision is the key to fulfilling your life's purpose.*

Chapter Principles

1. The poorest person in the world is a person without a dream.

2. The most frustrated person in the world is someone who has a dream but doesn't know how to make it come to pass.

3. Every person was created by God to be unique and distinct.

4. God has placed in every human being a unique vision and call that is designed to give purpose and meaning to life.

5. No person can give you your vision. It is God-given.

6. Every human being was created to accomplish something that no one else can accomplish.

7. Every person was created to be known for something special.

8. One person with vision is greater than the passive force of ninety-nine people who are merely interested in doing or becoming something.

9. Your gift will make a way for you in the world and enable you to fulfill your vision.

10. You are responsible for stirring up the gift within you.

11. God loves dreamers. He gives visions, and He is attracted to people who love to dream big.

12. As long as a person can hold on to his vision, then there is always a chance for him to move out of his present circumstances and toward the fulfillment of his purpose.

Chapter Two

The Source of Vision

VISION IS FORESIGHT WITH INSIGHT BASED ON HINDSIGHT.

T he first step to fulfilling your reason for existence is realizing that you have been given a vision. Yet how exactly do you receive, recognize, and activate your vision? When you understand the source of vision, you will learn the secrets to its origin and working in your life. This knowledge will help you take your dream from initial idea all the way to fulfillment.

Vision Comes from Purpose

The first key to understanding vision is to realize that it always emanates from purpose. Why? God is the Author of vision, and it is His nature to be purposeful in everything He does. Every time He appeared on the scene in human history, it was because He wanted something specific accomplished and was actively working it out through people's lives.

Therefore, God is a God of action based on purpose. Moreover, His purposes are eternal. Psalm 33:11 says, *"The plans of the LORD stand firm forever, the purposes of his heart through all generations,"* and Isaiah 14:24 says, *"The LORD Almighty has sworn, 'Surely, as I have planned, so it will be, and as I have purposed, so it will stand.'"* Nothing can get in the way of God's purposes; they always come to pass.

God Created You with a Purpose

Second, we must understand that God created everything to fulfill a purpose in life. Whether we are talking about a mammal, reptile, plant, star, or person, everything and everyone God created serves a unique purpose. That includes you. You may have been a surprise to your parents, but you were not a surprise to God; He has given you a special purpose to fulfill. The Scriptures say you were chosen in Him before the world began. (See Ephesians 1:4–5.) God planned in advance all that you were born to be and accomplish.

I am continually positive about life because I know that God created me for a purpose and that He will bring that purpose to pass. I believe that I'm not a mistake, and I know that my life is significant. God created me to do something, and no one else can do it for me. Do you believe that about yourself? Do you know that your life has a purpose? I hope you will become more and more confident of this truth as you progress through this book.

You Were Born at the Right Time

In the book of Ecclesiastes, we read about the revelation of God's purposes to the hearts of humankind. The third chapter begins, *"To everything there is a season, a time for every purpose under heaven"* (Ecclesiastes 3:1 NKJV). God has not only given you a purpose, but, according to this Scripture, He has also determined the time for that purpose to be accomplished. There is *"a time for every purpose."* Whatever you were born to do, God has assigned a season in which it is to be done—and that season is the duration of your life. Do you see why it is crucial for you to know the vision that is in your heart? Your purpose can be fulfilled only during the time you are given on earth to accomplish it.

Within this season called life, God has also appointed specific times for portions of your purpose to be accomplished. As you pursue the dream God has given you, He will bring it to fruition during the period of your life when it is meant to be completed. As Ecclesiastes 3:11 says, *"He has made everything beautiful in its time."*

Some people wish they had been born during a different time in history. Yet if you had been born a thousand years ago, or even a hundred years ago, you would have been miserable because you would have been living in the wrong time to complete your purpose and vision. God chose when and where you were born for a reason. You didn't just show up on earth. Ecclesiastes 3:2 says that there is *a time to be born.* **You were born at the right time to accomplish your vision during your generation.**

You Were Given a Sense of Purpose

Ecclesiastes 3:10 says, *"I have seen the burden God has laid on men."* The word *"burden"* in the Hebrew could actually be translated as "a heavy responsibility," "occupation," or "task." It could also be described as a "responsible urge." Every human being comes to earth with a purpose that, in a sense, weighs on him. Whether you are twenty, sixty, or ninety years old, there is a burden within you, a "responsible urge" to carry out all that you were designed to do. It is a cry of the heart—a cry of purpose that says, "I was born to do something that I must fulfill."

There is something within you that is being called by eternity.

Do you sense that cry? Do you feel that you were born to do something with your life? Almost everybody does, even if they have never expressed it. That feeling, longing, or burden comes from God. God has placed a "responsible urge" on your heart because of His purpose for you.

God Placed His Eternal Purpose in Your Heart

In Ecclesiastes 3:11, we read, *"He has also set eternity in the hearts of men."* That is a powerful statement. There is something within you that is being called by eternity. Unless we have turned a deaf ear to it, then every day we wake up hearing a call that comes from outside this world. We live in time and space, but time and space are connected to eternity, and God has put something into your heart that calls the unseen into the seen.

The vision God has put in your heart is "a piece of eternity" that He gave you to deliver in time and space—that is, on the earth during your lifetime. What God put into your heart is also what is in His own heart. I think this is what the Bible means when it talks about "deep calling unto deep." (See Psalm 42:7.)

43

Therefore, God has done something awesome. He lives in eternity, yet He has specifically placed you in time so that others on earth will be able to see a piece of eternity that is in Him.

It is this piece of eternity that makes you uncomfortable or dissatisfied with your present life because you are not yet manifesting your purpose.

Your Purpose Is Already Completed in God

The third key to understanding vision is realizing that not only has your purpose been given to you to manifest, but it has also been completed in eternity. The following passage entirely changed my perspective on the fulfillment of vision:

> *I am God, and there is no other; I am God, and there is none like me. I make known the end from the beginning, from ancient times, what is still to come. I say: My purpose will stand, and I will do all that I please.* (Isaiah 46:9–10)

In this Scripture, God mentions two things that He does. First, He establishes the end before the beginning. This means that He finishes things first in the spiritual realm, and then He goes back and starts them up in the physical realm. Second, He reveals the end result of something when it is just beginning.

I have noticed in the Scriptures the principle that purpose is established before production. In other words, God first institutes a purpose, then He creates someone or something to fulfill that purpose. He is the Alpha and the Omega, the beginning and the end. We often don't recognize the fact that when God starts something, He has already completed it in eternity. *"Yet they cannot fathom what God has done from beginning to end"* (Ecclesiastes 3:11). We need to remember His order of working: He first tells us what the end of the matter is to be, and then He backs up and begins the process of fulfilling that end—just as a builder first develops an idea and a blueprint and then starts building.

We can see this principle in Creation. Everything was already finished in God's mind before He laid the foundation of the world. After He had imagined and planned how He wanted everything to be, *then* He initiated the beginning by creating the heavens, the earth, and humankind. In the book of Genesis, which means "origin" or "source," we are really reading about the start-up of the project called "earth." Those of you who are involved in project management know that start-up is a significant step in the process of building. When you reach the start-up phase, it means that you have all the plans drawn, all the physical resources in place, and all the management resources in order. Before you start a project, all these things must be in place. Only *then* can you begin.

When do you start building a house? Is it when you dig the foundation? Essentially, you begin building whenever the idea for the house is conceived. The finished house is still in the unseen; other people pass by the property, and they don't see it. However, to you, who understand and know what is going to happen, the house is already finished. Digging the foundation is simply the beginning of bringing your purpose to pass. Therefore, after you dig the foundation, and somebody asks you, "What are you doing?" your answer is very definite. You point to the architect's rendering of the house and say, "I am building this."

Purpose is established before production.

There is a street near where I live called Shirley Street. At one time, there was a parking lot there. One day when I was driving along that street, I saw a large sign with a beautifully painted picture of a building. There was no building on the site yet, but there was the big sign and the name of the building. It showed the landscape, the color of the building, the windows, everything; it was a very detailed picture of what the completed building would look like. The sign said, "Coming soon."

I drove past the lot and sensed God saying to me, "Did you see that?" I said, "See what?" He said, "Did you see the finish?" So I turned my car around and went back to take a closer look at the sign. By showing the completed picture of the building, the construction company was revealing the end of its purpose. To have vision means to see something coming into view as if it were already there. The company had a vision for that building because it saw the finished product before construction had even begun.

God essentially completed us before He created us. Not only does He establish our ends, but He also gives us glimpses of them through the visions He puts in our hearts. We must pay attention to His work within us so that we will be able to understand more of what He *"has done from beginning to end"* (Ecclesiastes 3:11).

Your Beginning Is Proof of Your Completion

God wants you to "see" the completion of your vision by knowing that He already planned and established it before you were born. The fact that you were started is proof that you are already completed because God always finishes before He starts and accomplishes His purposes. Therefore, instead of striving to fulfill what God has given you to do, you can rely on Him to finish it as you allow Him to guide you in the specifics of carrying it out.

Vision means to see something coming into view as if it were already there.

For example, as I move forward in the development of Bahamas Faith Ministries International, I am not trying to "finish" it. God has already completed a world-class center for leadership training in all its facets, including the Third World Leaders Association and Leading Edge Leadership. He finished it in eternity, and now He is bringing it to pass. He purposed it, and then He backed up and said, "Now let me go to a little island in the Bahamas and prompt a young man who lives in a little wooden house in a family of eleven kids so he can start the process of completing the vision." The process is God's way of preparing me and those involved in BFMI for the end result.

You are not an experiment. God wouldn't have allowed you to start your life and your purpose unless they were already completed in eternity. You were born to manifest something that is already finished. You must realize, however, that your end doesn't look anything like your beginning—or like any other point in the process, for that matter. This is why you must live by faith, looking forward with expectation for what God has already completed; otherwise, you will believe only what you see with your physical eyes rather than the vision you see in your heart.

At this point, I want to clarify the difference between purpose and vision. Purpose is the intent for which God created you, the reason why you were born. Purpose is what God has already decided in His own mind that you're supposed to begin to fulfill. Therefore,

- **purposeiswhenyouknowandunderstandwhatyou were born to accomplish, and**
- **visioniswhenyoucanseeitinyourmindbyfaith and begin to imagine it.**

When you are able to see your purpose, your vision comes to life.

I like this definition: "Vision is foresight with insight based on hindsight." We have insight into God's purpose for us based on what we know God has already accomplished in eternity. **Vision is a glimpse of our future that God has purposed.** We don't know all the details of how our purposes will unfold, but we see their "ends" because God reveals them to us in the visions He gives us. This is why we can be confident that they will come to pass.

Suppose you don't have the money you need to fulfill your vision. God says to you, in effect, "I've already been where you are going, and you will have everything you need." He tells us that our visions will be completed, and this is what gives us courage and keeps us from being depressed when things don't look as if they will work out.

You Were Designed Perfectly to Complete Your Purpose

When God created you with a purpose, He also designed you perfectly to be able to fulfill it. This means He wired you in a specific way so that you would have all the essential components necessary for fulfilling the vision He gave you. You never have to worry if you are able to fulfill your life's vision. The fact that you were created to complete it means that you have everything you need to accomplish it. God always gives us the ability to do whatever He calls us to do.

Vision Is about God

Purpose, therefore, is the source of your vision. Your purpose existed before you did. What you were born to do was accomplished by God before you even arrived on the scene, and He ordained your birth in order to carry it out. God did not create you and then say, "Let Me see what I can do with this one." He doesn't create something and then decide what to use it for. He knows what He wants first, and then He assigns someone or something to accomplish it for Him.

Vision is not our private view of the future but the view of our future inspired by God.

Consequently, at its essence, vision isn't about us—it's about God. Proverbs 19:21 says, *"Many are the plans in a man's heart, but it is the Lord's purpose that prevails."* True vision is not a human invention. It's about the desires God imparts to us. It is not our private view of the future; rather, it is the view of our future inspired by God. Vision is what God wants us to contribute in building His kingdom on earth. His purpose was established well before we had any plans for our lives. We were meant to consult God to find out His purposes for us so we can make the right plans. Ecclesiastes 3:14 says, *"I know that everything God does will endure forever; nothing can be added to it and nothing taken from it. God does it so that men will revere him."*

You Already Know Your Vision

Fourth, we must understand the key to recognizing personal vision. After reading my books on purpose, many people write to me and say, "Okay, I read your book. It's wonderful, it changed my life, and I'm ready to go, except that I don't know what my vision is. Tell me how to find it." To find your vision, you have to look within yourself, where God has placed it. The key is this: God's will is as close to us as our most persistent thoughts and deepest desires.

Vision Is as Close as Your Deepest Desires

Psalm 37:4 says, *"Delight yourself in the LORD and he will give you the desires of your...."* Desires of your what? *"Your heart"* (v. 4). Wait a minute. Doesn't God give us desires from heaven? Yes, He does. Our desires originated there, but remember that God has placed His desires for you within your heart. He put the plans for your life within you when you were born, and they have never left you. The heart, in this case, means your subconscious mind. God put His plans there because He wants to make sure you find them. Sometimes, His ideas come in multiples. God may put five or six things in your mind that He wants you to do, each one for a different season of your life.

Yet whether He gives you one idea or six ideas, the thoughts of God are consistent. They will be present throughout your life. No matter how old you grow, the same thoughts will keep coming back to you, and the desires will never leave you. This is because the will of God for you never changes. The Bible says, *"God's gifts and his call are irrevocable"* (Romans 11:29). The specifics of your plans may change as your purpose unfolds, but your purpose is permanent. No matter what happens in life, you'll never get away from what God has put in your heart to do. **Vision possesses you; you don't possess it.**

All the thoughts, ideas, plans, and dreams that remain consistent within you were put there by God. No matter how many times you may temporarily forget about them, they always come back into your mind. Vision is the idea that never leaves you, the dream that won't go away, the passion that won't subside, the "irritating" desire that's so deep you can't enjoy your current job because you're always thinking about what you wish you were doing. Vision is what you keep seeing, even when you close your eyes.

I have found that people are constantly waiting for God to tell them what to do when it has been given to them already. Religious people, especially Christian people, have been looking for God's will everywhere except within themselves. It's necessary for them to realize that they don't receive their purposes after they are born again; they were already given their purposes when they were physically born. God has saved us because He gave us assignments that He doesn't want to lose. You're not saved for the sole purpose of going to heaven; you're saved to finish your assignment on earth. As a matter of fact, God redeems you because of the vision you are carrying. The Bible says, *"We are God's workmanship, created in Christ Jesus to do good works, which God **prepared in advance** for us to do"* (Ephesians 2:10, emphasis added).

Many people have been looking for God's will everywhere except in themselves.

Many people ask me how God speaks to us. They say, "I want to hear from God. Does He speak in an audible voice? Does He come in the night and whisper in my ear? Does He speak through some animal or write on the wall like He did in the Old Testament?" They don't realize that God has been speaking to them since they were born, and He is still speaking to them now. He speaks to them through the thoughts, ideas, and visions they keep having in their minds. If you are unclear about your vision, you can ask God to reveal to you the deepest desires He has placed within you.

Some people call psychic hot lines to get others to tell them their futures. You don't need to consult psychics or read tarot cards. The sad thing is that some Christians do nearly the equivalent of this when they run from meeting to meeting, asking people to prophesy over them concerning their futures, not understanding that God has given them their visions directly. A prophet can *confirm* your vision, but he or she will not *give* you your vision. God gives you that directly, and He reveals it to you as you listen to

Him and follow Him. God says, *"If you had responded to my rebuke, I would have poured out my heart to you and made my thoughts known to you"* (Proverbs 1:23), and *"I will put my law in their minds and write it on their hearts"* (Jeremiah 31:33). God puts His thoughts within us through the Holy Spirit. What we have to do is listen to what God has given us in our hearts and minds.

Vision Is Much More than Mere "Interest"

One way to discern whether something is a vision from God is to determine whether you have a real desire to do it or merely a passing interest in it. You can be interested in something, yet not really have a passion to do it. If you have passion, though, you will actively pursue your vision and things will start happening to bring it to pass. Remember that one person with vision is greater than the passive force of ninety-nine people who are merely interested in doing or becoming something.

Vision Will Persist against the Odds

Another way to recognize true vision is when you persevere in your dream regardless of great obstacles. When many people think about their dreams, they say, "Oh, no, that's impossible for me to do," so they settle down to do something lesser and end up being unfulfilled. The problem is often that we have been trained and brainwashed by our societies to dream small, think small, expect small, and not try to do anything too big. When we compare what we are told to see in the "real" world with our own dreams, our visions seem unrealistic and start to fade away. Yet if a vision is truly from God, we are meant to continue on, no matter what the difficulty. Therefore, if you have a genuine vision from God, you will need to develop persistence, which we'll talk more about in a later chapter.

Vision Is Unselfish

True vision is also unselfish. Its purpose is to bring about God's kingdom on earth and to turn people to Him. **A vision, therefore, should always focus on helping humanity or building up others in some way.**

This means, first of all, that God will never have you pursue your vision at the expense of your family. An older man, who is a very beloved friend of mine, went to a conference, and a supposed prophet spoke to him about what God wanted for his life. He came to me afterward and said, "Did you hear what the prophet said?" I said, "Yes." He asked, "What do you think?" I replied, "Well, let's pray over that prophecy. Let's take our time, get counsel, and find God's will on it." The next time I heard from him, he had already set up a plan to fulfill this prophecy. He left his family and went to another country. Was this really God's purpose?

There are instances when members of a family will agree to be apart *for a time* in order to serve a certain purpose. However, this was not the case with this man. When he pursued this prophecy, his wife was frustrated and his children were confused and angered. He was breaking up his family and causing all kinds of problems and difficulties for them.

A true vision will always build others up rather than pull them down.

If pursuing your vision is causing turmoil in your family, stop and do some serious praying and soul-searching about the situation. Talk with your family members and listen to what they have to say. While you can expect to face some opposition to your vision, and while your family will not always understand or support your dream, pursuing it shouldn't destroy the lives of your loved ones. **Vision should always be accompanied by compassion.** You need to be careful and sensitive not to hurt anyone on the way to achieving your goal.

The second thing we should be aware of in regard to the unselfish nature of vision is that a true vision will not take the form of building a big business just so you can have millions of dollars, an expensive home, a sleek car, and a vacation house on the beach. These things are goals, but they are not vision—in fact, they are probably selfish ambition. Why? Because they build your kingdom rather than God's kingdom. Your vision might well involve making a large amount of money. The difference, however, is in your motivation and attitude toward the money. Your perspective on your finances should be God-centered, not self-centered. You need to treat your finances as a resource God has provided to fulfill your vision, not as a tool to fill your life with luxuries.

Vision Is the Only Thing That Will Bring You Fulfillment

Another way you can know that a vision is real is when it is the only thing that gives you true satisfaction. Merely working at a job is disheartening. Going to work is a dismal experience for many people because, day after day, they are doing something they hate. That is not what you were meant for. Ecclesiastes 3:13 says, *"That everyone may eat and drink, and find satisfaction in all his toil—this is the gift of God."* It is God's desire for us to enjoy our work, but this can happen only when we're doing the right work.

Therefore, until you follow God's dream, you will be unfulfilled. Proverbs 19:21 says, *"Many are the plans in a man's heart, but it is the Lord's purpose that prevails."* No matter what you are busy doing, no matter what you are accomplishing, if it's not what God wants you to do, you won't be completely successful in it. Why? Because true success is not in what you accomplish; it is in doing what God told you to do. That's why people who build big projects or gain great fame can be successful and depressed at the same time.

Going against your purpose may be a personal issue, but it's never a private one. You can mess up others' lives if you aren't supposed to be where you are, or if you are supposed to be somewhere that you refuse to go. Remember the story of Jonah in the Bible? God told him that his purpose was to go to Nineveh to warn the people there to turn to God. Jonah's response was, in effect, "I'm not going!" He got on a ship headed for Tarshish, instead.

God had purposed that Jonah would go to Nineveh even before the prophet was born. His purpose had already been completed in eternity, and now God was sending him to fulfill it. God didn't want Jonah to be on a ship going to Tarshish when he was meant to go to Nineveh. If you get on any other "ship" than the one you were meant to get on, you are going to cause others to have problems. In Jonah's case, the ship he got on came in danger of sinking in a terrible storm. He knew God's hand was in the situation, so he told the sailors that the storm would stop if they would throw him overboard. When the sailors did this, the sea became calm, and God provided a great fish to swallow Jonah—protecting him from the sea until he agreed to do what God had called him to do. (See Jonah 1–2.)

I urge you not to board the wrong ship, but to remain on course in God's purpose. Maybe you're in the fish's belly right now. You can find your way back to dry land by returning to what God has purposed for you to do.

Going against your purpose may be personal but it's never private.

Vision Requires a Vital Connection with God

Many people don't recognize the vision God has placed within them because they don't have a vital connection with God. This connection with Him needs to be restored before they can see their true purpose. Humankind as a whole lost its relationship with the Creator when man and woman turned their backs on God and tried to pursue their own ways. God's purpose, however, never changes, and since His purpose is woven into our desires, our own ways are never ultimately satisfying.

God is committed to your purpose, and He provided salvation through Christ to salvage His will and purpose in your life. He said, in effect, "I'm not going to lose what I gave you birth to do. I'm going to save you for your own sake and so I can redeem what I want to accomplish through you." He restores us to Himself so we can do the works He had in mind for us before the world began. Again, *"we are God's workmanship, created in Christ Jesus to do good works, which God prepared in advance for us to do"* (Ephesians 2:10). **We are not saved by doing good works but for the purpose of doing good works.**

In other words, we are saved to fulfill our earthly visions. If we are saved just so that we can go to heaven, then God is taking a long time to accomplish His plan. The quickest way to heaven is death. If God wanted us in heaven immediately, He would save us and then cause us to die the next day. God wants us to accomplish the purposes He's given us to fulfill on earth; that is why He saves us, sanctifies us, and keeps us here for a time.

Once we are restored to God, we receive His Holy Spirit and can see and understand the vision He has placed in our hearts. We learn to discern true vision through our relationship with Him and by reading His Word, because genuine vision is always in alignment with His nature and character. The Bible says, *"Casting down imaginations, and every high thing that exalteth itself against the knowledge of God"* (2 Corinthians 10:5 KJV). This verse is talking about ideas. It continues, *"Bringing into captivity every thought to the obedience of Christ."* Any idea that isn't contrary to the Word of God, or to obedience to Christ's wishes for your life, is a God idea. God ideas are always in agreement with His will. God would never give you an idea that is contrary to the Bible. That is impossible. Therefore, you are to cast down any ideas that are contrary to His Word. You are to ignore them. If an idea is not in keeping with God's will, set it aside.

Corporate Vision and Personal Vision

The fifth key to understanding vision is to realize that it is both personal and corporate; personal vision will always be found within a larger corporate vision. It is not God's method to give a vision to a group. He gives the vision to an individual who shares his vision with the group and transfers it to them. The members of the group then run with the vision because they find in it a place for their own personal visions to be fulfilled.

55

Moses was constrained by a vision to deliver the people of Israel and lead them to the Promised Land. Joshua was motivated by a vision to possess that land. David was driven by a vision to settle God's people. Nehemiah was possessed by a vision to rebuild the walls of Jerusalem. In every case, the vision was given to an individual who was ultimately responsible for seeing it through, and the individual transferred it to a group.

Working Together to Fulfill the Vision

When a person starts to sense his purpose and gift, he often interprets this as a call to autonomy and separation. However, nothing could be further from the truth. A sense of personal vision is birthed within a broader vision, and it will also be fulfilled in the context of a larger purpose. This is how God weaves personal and corporate vision together. In order to accomplish a corporate purpose or make a larger vision come to pass, God brings together many people's personal gifts and unique visions. God wants you to bring your time, energy, resources, and creative power to be part of a larger vision to which your vision is connected.

We know that a car functions only when all the parts of the engine are working together. Although each part has its unique characteristics and private functions, all the parts "submit" to one another to make the car run. The same principle holds true for corporate and personal vision. **No great work was ever done by just one person. Many people are needed to fulfill a vision.** Read history. Read the Bible.

A group of men, for example, supported and helped Dr. Martin Luther King, Jr., in fulfilling his vision. We all know Dr. King's name, but we hear very little about these other men, even though they were essential to his purpose. Dr. King could not have fulfilled his vision without their assistance. Likewise, we don't know the names of those who helped Moses judge and arbitrate between the people of Israel, but they were an essential support element in the purpose of leading the people that God had given Moses. Those men worked hard. They had to execute judgment and keep everyone in order, yet we know only Moses' name. Moses received a personal vision, but all these men were needed to see the corporate vision through. (See Exodus 18:13–26.) **God will bring together private purposes and visions in order to facilitate corporate success.**

When people don't understand or accept the relationship between personal and corporate vision, there can be problems. If the members of the group think they are inferior to the person with the original vision, or the leader starts to think he is more important than the members, or if one or more of the members wants to supplant the person who has the larger vision, that is when the trouble will begin. Moses had the latter problem with Miriam and Aaron, his sister and brother. God had appointed them all as leaders. (See Micah 6:4.) Moses, however, was the one who had received the original vision, and he was the one with whom God met directly and through whom God spoke. When Miriam and Aaron became jealous of Moses and wanted to usurp his role, it caused turmoil within that leadership group. God had to remind Miriam and Aaron in a very graphic way that it is His purposes that prevail, not our private ambitions. (See Numbers 12:4–15.) However, if we are in line with God's nature and character, we will desire what He desires, and we will be fulfilled in a way we never could have been by following our own ambitions.

Personal vision will always be found within a larger corporate vision.

We must have an attitude of cooperation with those with whom we share corporate vision. Fulfilling your vision requires your being able to submit to others in the larger purpose. It means working with your boss and coworkers in a productive way. It means not trying to undermine the leaders of your group or letting jealousy get in the way of the vision. It means not going off and trying to fulfill a corporate vision all on your own. If we are going to do something for God so that the world will be better off because we were here, we can't do that with a private, individualist attitude. It is important for us to be cautious when we're dealing with vision. Let us be cognizant of God's ways and work with them rather than against them.

Drawing Out the Vision

When we understand the relationship between personal and corporate vision, we will know a chief way in which God fulfills people's dreams. Proverbs 20:5 says, *"The purposes of a man's heart are* [like] *deep waters, but a man of understanding draws them out."* In other words, everyone has a vision in his heart, but a person of understanding causes that dream, that purpose, that vision to be brought out so it can become reality. A person of understanding will figuratively lower a bucket into the deep well-waters of your soul and begin to draw out what you are dreaming and thinking. He will give life to your desires and thoughts and thereby help make them a reality.

No great work was ever done by just one person.

What is the process by which this occurs? After God conveys a vision to a leader, you will then—in one way or another—come into contact with this person, who will present the corporate vision, and you will become excited about participating in it because you will see how your private vision finds fulfillment in it. It is essential for you to understand that God brings the corporate vision into your life not to *give* you vision, which He has already given you, but to *stir up* your personal vision. **In other words, you don't receive your vision from other people, but you are enabled to fulfill it through others.** The leader of the corporate vision helps to activate your passions, dreams, gifts, and talents.

In a sense, that is what I hope to do through this book. It is my desire to stir up your vision. As I wrote earlier, my own vision is to inspire and draw out the hidden leader in every person I meet. You are a leader in the specific purpose God has given you to accomplish through your gift because no one else but you can fulfill it. I hope my vision of your potential for leadership will excite and motivate you to fulfill the vision in your heart. Perhaps something has already begun to happen within you. Are you starting to think differently? Are you beginning to dream? Are you able to believe in the possibility of things you never thought possible before? Then you have started to catch the vision for your life.

We must cooperate with those with whom we share corporate vision.

The corporate vision in which your personal vision will ultimately be fulfilled might be that of a company, a church, a non-profit organization, or even your own family. That is why, when you hear of something that is related to your vision, you should pay attention to it, because it may be that you're supposed to attach yourself to it. You yourself may be given the corporate vision, such as starting a business or organizing a community project. Yet none of us is meant to complete our visions on our own. **The joy of God's plan for personal and corporate vision is that nothing we are born to do is to be done by ourselves or for ourselves.** If you and I are part of the same corporate vision, then I need your vision, and you need mine. Therefore, we must stay together and work together. We are not to isolate ourselves in our private successes.

I'm not involved in the work that I'm doing to build a name for myself. My life's work is to complete the assignment God gave me. Every member of my staff and organization has a part to play in our vision. My part is to stir up their individual dreams, and their part is to stir up mine. When we stir up each other's visions, the divine deposit of destiny starts flowing. Vision generates vision. Dreams always stir up other dreams.

Whenever I begin to feel discouraged, I always telephone my friends who have big dreams. One day, I called my friend Peter Morgan. When he heard my voice, he said, "What's going on?"

I said, "I just called to talk to you." He said, "What's wrong?" "Nothing; just talk to me." "What do you mean?" "Just talk to me. Tell me what you are going to do with your life. Tell me where you are headed. Let me know I'm not alone in pursuing a vision."

Corporate vision is not meant to *give* you vision but to *stir up* your personal vision.

You need people around you who believe in dreams that are even bigger than your own so you can keep stirring up your vision. There are too many other people who will tell you to settle down and do nothing. Yet a person of understanding will stir up your purposes. A person of understanding will cause your dream to rise from that deep well within you and will help you make real progress toward your vision. You'll begin to believe that, no matter where you came from, where you're going is better.

Action Steps to Fulfilling Vision

- Take half an hour and allow yourself to dream about what you would like to do in life. What ideas and desires do you have? What have you always wanted to do?

- Think about your primary gifts or talents. How do your dreams and your gifts go together?

- Write down your ideas, desires, and gifts and read them over every evening for a week. Then ask yourself, "Do these ideas hold true? Are they what I want to do?" If the answer is yes, keep them where you can refer to them as you read this book and watch them form into a specific vision and concrete goals that will move you along toward the completion of your purpose.

Chapter Principles

1. Vision comes from purpose.

2. God created everything and everyone with a purpose.

3. God has placed His eternal purpose in your heart.

4. You were given a burden or "responsible urge" to complete your purpose.

5. You were born at the right time to fulfill your purpose.

6. Your purpose is already completed in God.

7. God completed you before He created you.

8. The fact that you were started is proof that you are completed.

9. You were designed to perfectly accomplish your purpose.

10. When you know and understand what you were born to accomplish, that is purpose. When you can see it in your mind by faith, that is vision.

11. Vision is foresight with insight based on hindsight.

12. Vision isn't about us. It's about God and His purposes.

13. You already know your vision. It is as close as your most persistent thoughts and deepest desires.

14. To have vision is to have more than a mere interest in something; it is to have a real desire and passion for it.

15. Vision persists, no matter what the odds.

16. Vision is unselfish.

17. Vision is the only thing that brings true fulfillment.

18. Vision requires a vital connection with God.

19. Personal vision will always be found within a larger corporate vision.

20. Those who are in the same corporate vision must work together harmoniously to achieve it.

21. The leader of corporate vision "draws out" the personal visions of those in the group by helping them to activate their passions, dreams, gifts, and talents.

22. Vision generates vision.

Chapter Three

Overcoming Obstacles
to Vision

MEDIOCRITY IS A REGION BORDERED ON THE NORTH BY COMPROMISE,
ON THE SOUTH BY INDECISION, ON THE EAST BY PAST THINKING, AND
ON THE WEST BY A LACK OF VISION.
—JOHN MASON

U nderstanding the source of vision is the first step in the process of fulfilling it. The next step is to be aware of potential obstacles in your life that can derail your vision. If you are aware of these obstacles ahead of time, you will be prepared to recognize and overcome them. Three major obstacles to fulfilling vision are

1. not understanding the nature of vision
2. not recognizing the cost of vision
3. not knowing the principles of vision

Most people live in mediocrity—a "region bordered on the north by compromise, on the south by indecision, on the east by past thinking, and on the west by a lack of vision." This chapter will show you how to leave behind the region of mediocrity and move into the realm of the exceptional.

Not Understanding the Nature of Vision

The main thing about vision is that it is *specific.* One of the greatest causes of failure among people who are pursuing their visions is that they don't identify their objective of success.

This may sound simple, but it is very true: People fail because they don't know what they want to succeed in. Much of our frustration and depression comes from not making any headway toward achieving our visions—even when we know we're working hard. This inability to reach our visions occurs when we don't aim at a specific target.

Suppose I came to you and said, "Let's meet." You say, "Okay; where?" I reply, "Oh, anywhere." You ask, "Well, *when* do you want to meet?" and I say, "Anytime." What do you think are the chances that we will actually meet? Practically zero. Vision must be specific rather than general or vague.

Misunderstanding the Difference between Vision, Goals, and Mission

I have asked many people, "What are you going to do with your life? What is your vision?" and I usually receive responses such as these: "I'm going to build a big house, own several cars, and have a good family." "I want to get married." "I want to open a restaurant someday." These are not visions, but mere goals.

People fail because they don't know what they want to succeed in.

When I ask pastors the same question, they generally give me one of the following answers: "My vision is to win my city to Christ." "My vision is to *'preach the gospel to every creature'* (Mark 16:15 KJV)." "Our vision as a church is to know Him and to make Him known." "Our vision is to equip people for the work of the ministry."

None of the above answers are visions. They are *missions*. Why? They are too general for visions. Vision and mission are related, but they are not the same thing. **A mission is a general statement of purpose that declares the overall idea of what you want to accomplish.** It is philosophical and abstract, not practical and concrete. Moreover, it is open-ended, so that you could spend hours, even days, talking about its many aspects and applications. In contrast, a vision is a very precise statement that has a specific emphasis and definable boundaries.

I sometimes wonder how some people have made it as far as they have without understanding vision. It is essential that you learn the difference between vision and mission because God is not vague about your life. You were designed to be unique and to fulfill a particular purpose. If you are to carry out this specific purpose, your vision has to be specific. Otherwise, you will be just like everyone else around you. Remember, your vision—like your fingerprints—is meant to distinguish you from every other person in the world.

Let me use the Christian church as an example. The assignment that the young Jewish rabbi, Jesus, gave His followers two thousand years ago—"*Go into all the world and preach the good news*" (Mark 16:15)—is called the Great Commission. It is the "co-mission," the joint or corporate mission of the church. It is every Christian's mission. What sincere church does not want to preach the Gospel to every person, bring people to God, and equip people to minister to others? Therefore, if a church thinks its particular vision is to preach the Gospel, then it has a mistaken idea of vision. It knows its *mission*, but it hasn't yet found its true *vision*, that one thing that distinguishes it from all other churches.

One church is not assigned where another church is assigned. That is why an individual church shouldn't compare itself with other churches in its city or nation or use another church as a measure of its own success. Vision is a distinctive direction or approach for accomplishing a mission. There is a unique way in which God wants each church to carry out the overall mission of the Great Commission. Each church is to fulfill its part of the mission through the specific emphasis or approach that God has given it. The same general principle holds true for individuals, companies, and other organizations.

One time a woman came to me and said, "Dr. Munroe, I have a vision. I'm going to open up a shoe store." I said, "Fine." Then she said, "There are already so many shoe stores in this area, but I know the Lord has told me that I must go into this business." I asked her, "What kind of shoes do you want to sell?" She said, "I want to sell only children's and babies' shoes." When I heard that, I told her, "Then you understand vision. Those other stores sell all kinds of adult shoes, but your store will be unique. When anyone wants children's shoes or babies' shoes, they're going to walk right past those other stores. They're going to look for you."

When you've discovered your own vision, you do not need to be jealous of anyone.

When you truly understand the difference between mission and vision, you will be protected from jealousy. You won't become sidetracked from your purpose by constantly looking over your shoulder to see what others who share your mission are doing. Let's return to the analogy of the Christian church. Although every church in the world is in the same business of "discipling the nations," if someone were to build a church right next to another church, a big fight might ensue. The first church might say, "This is my territory. God gave me this neighborhood. Get your church out of here." The members of the two churches might end up suspicious of one another, fighting all the time and putting each other down. That is what happens when churches don't understand vision.

When you've discovered your own vision, however, you do not need to be jealous of anyone because there's no need for competition. This truth was demonstrated to me in a very tangible way. One day, I was talking with a man who owns the McDonald's franchise in the Bahamas. While we were talking, the owner of the Kentucky Fried Chicken franchise stopped by. He introduced himself to me, and I said, "It's good to meet you." I was curious, so I added, "What are you doing here?" He gestured toward my friend and said, "We're going to have lunch together." I decided to go with them, because I wanted to see where they would end up eating. They went to Pizza Hut!

I sat at a table eating pizza with them and observing them while they talked. Finally, I said, "Excuse me, gentlemen. First of all, aren't you competitors?" They both said, "No." I asked, "What do you mean?" My friend answered, "He doesn't sell what I sell. I don't sell what he sells. How can we be in competition?" Then I said, "Second question. Why did you come here?" He replied, "We didn't feel like eating burgers or chicken. We felt like eating pizza!"

There is a place for all three establishments because each restaurant has its own specific vision. Each offers a different product in the overall mission of serving food. Businesses, organizations, churches, and individuals can learn the true nature of vision from the example of these two men.

I travel around the world and speak at large churches alongside well-known pastors. Sometimes, I notice certain approaches or methods that their churches are using. I see that people gravitate to certain ministries, and I'm tempted to imitate them, thinking, "I should try that. Maybe I can get more people to come if I do what they do." Yet the Lord says to me, "Don't you dare." If I try to imitate others, I won't be fulfilling the specific purpose and vision He has given me, and I will no longer have His full blessing. He says, in effect, "I'm not going to bless what you create. I'm going to bless what I create."

We must be true to our own visions. Each of us must measure the success of our visions by God's assignment to us. We need to ask ourselves this question: "Am I doing what God told me to do?"

Engaging in Wishful Thinking

Another reason people aren't specific about their visions is that they're caught in a trap of wishful thinking. Their dreaming doesn't go beyond vague ideas of what they would like to do "someday." Yet dreaming is only the beginning of vision. We should have wills rather than mere wishes. In other words, instead of wishing that things would get better, we must make concrete resolutions. We have to say, "Things *must* get better, and here, specifically, is what I'm going to do about it." For example, instead of saying, "I wish I could go to college," sit down today, write specific colleges with requests for applications, and when they arrive, start filling them out. Instead of saying, "I wish I could lose weight," see your doctor and go on a specific weight-loss plan. Make a decision, and then take the first step.

We should have wills rather than mere wishes.

People's success or failure in life is not dependent on the color of their skin. You can be black, white, brown, yellow, or red, and that won't affect the fulfillment of your vision. The real problem is the color of some people's *lives*; their lives are "gray." Such people don't have a precise way of living. They're just here. They drift along, allowing life to happen to them.

God doesn't want anyone to live in a gray zone. When someone is living in the gray, it means that person is not saying yes or no, but maybe. He never quite settles on one thing in his heart. There are millions of people who still aren't sure who they are, what they're about, and what they're doing. These people are living in the gray. They have no real intention of doing anything with their lives. What a depressing reality. God has invested so much in us. He hates to see us wasting our lives in wishful thinking. He wants us to place our feet on the solid ground of vision.

Living with Indecision

Many people's visions never take specific shape because they can't make up their minds what they want to do in life. The only decision they make is *not* to decide. Prolonged indecisiveness is a vision-killer, and it also drains the joy out of life. I've noticed that the most miserable people in the world are those who can never make a decision. The Bible expresses their situation well: *"A double minded man is unstable in **all** his ways"* (James 1:8 KJV, emphasis added). Indecisiveness carries over into all areas of life. A person who is indecisive is unsettled; he's on shaky ground.

Prolonged indecisiveness is a vision-killer.

Many of us make shopping lists before we go to the store, but few of us make lists of what we want for our lives. As I said in chapter one, many people—perhaps yourself— have been trying to decide to do something for years, yet they still haven't made a solid decision about it. Sometimes, they impose this delay on themselves because of uncertainty or fear of failure; other times they worry about what other people might say or think about their ideas. Yet these people are putting themselves in a dangerous position: the middle of the road. When you are indecisive, life keeps running you over.

I am committed to fulfilling what God gave me birth to do. I resolved years ago that I would look only to God's Word and the vision He put in my heart to know what I could accomplish. In this way, God's purposes and principles have determined what I'm going to be and do rather than my own fears or others' opinions. I am set on my vision, just as Jesus was set on His. The Bible says, *"Now it came to pass, when the time had come for [Jesus] to be received up, that He steadfastly set His face to go to Jerusalem"* (Luke 9:51 NKJV). Jesus set His face *"steadfastly"* or *"like flint"* (Isaiah 50:7) in His determination to fulfill His purpose. Flint is one of the hardest rocks you can find. This analogy means that after Jesus had set His goal to go to the cross, it was too late to talk Him out of it. He was set and determined to accomplish His vision.

Are you living that way? Is there something you have decided to follow through with, no matter what? Are you committed to a vision that is bigger than your life?

Making Excuses

Sometimes, we know what we should be doing, but we're hesitant to take that first step. We always intend to do it, but we never do. Instead, we make excuses, such as "When my life gets less complicated," "When I feel more confident," or "After I pray about it more."

There is a story of two fishermen who were lost in a storm on a lake. The storm was blowing so fiercely that they couldn't see a thing. One of the fishermen said to his colleague, "We have two choices. We can pray or row. Which one should we do?" The other answered, "Let's do both!" That's the way you need to live. Instead of deliberating about what you need to do, just say, "Let's row." Even though you're scared, keep on rowing. Set a destination even while you're praying, and God will guide you where you need to go.

Another group of people who have trouble carrying vision through to the end is what I call the "professional starters." They're always beginning something, but they never finish anything. For example, they have books they've never finished, yet they keep starting new ones. Nothing in the world feels as good as reading through to the last page of a book because then you know that that book is in you and no one can take it away from you. Everything you leave unfinished will discourage you from completing other projects. The unfinished has a way of haunting your life.

Seeking "Balance"

Some people don't want to focus on a specific goal because they fear their lives might not be well-balanced. They say things such as these: "I don't really want to go after anything in particular because then I will be closing off other options. I don't want to become too narrow," or "If I become too serious about something, I might miss what I really want to do in life." The problem is that people will say things like these for forty-five years and never end up doing anything at all! What they call a pursuit of balance is really an excuse for not making a decision. They end up being average, mediocre people.

Are you committed to a vision that is bigger than your life?

True balance is the maintenance of equilibrium while moving toward a destination. A good example of this truth is the way a ship functions on the ocean. A ship always needs to maintain its balance. Wouldn't it be a waste of precious time and fuel, however, for a boat to expend all its energy just trying to balance on the water so that it didn't tip over? Some people live for sixty-five years, seventy-five years, ninety years, just balancing. Yet balance is not an end in itself; it is a means to an end. A ship keeps its balance as it makes its way to a specific port. Likewise, we need to have a destination while we're maintaining balance in our lives.

Trying to Do Everything

A common reason people aren't specific about their visions is that they're trying to do too much. Their problem isn't that they're hesitant about getting started, but that they're running around attempting too many things. Even though they are constantly constructing something, they're actually building nothing at all because they never complete anything.

Why does this happen? Because most people make the mistake of believing that the main goal in life is to stay busy. Yet this way of thinking is a trap. Busyness does not necessarily equal progress; staying busy does not necessarily mean that you are heading toward a specific destination.

I have learned this very important truth that has set me free from both indecision and ineffective busyness: *I was not born or created to do everything.* This statement might be a good thing to put at the top of your office or household calendar. When we aim at everything, we usually hit nothing. Yet most

71

of us are breaking our necks trying to hit everything in sight. Let me assure you: You were not born to meet all the needs on earth.

It is very easy to become concerned about the many problems we face in this world. Compassion is not only an admirable quality, but it is also an essential element of vision. However, you cannot try to meet every need around you and still be effective in helping people. The more needs you attempt to meet, the less attention you'll be able to devote to each individual need.

You were not born to do everything.

All the needs that you see in your nation cannot be met by you. *All* the trouble that you see in your community cannot be solved by you. *All* the problems that you see on your street cannot be addressed by you. This reality is the reason why you must discover your personal vision from God and then stay on track with it. You were meant to meet certain needs, not every need. God created you for a purpose, and that purpose is supposed to be your focus. It is what must motivate you and keep you centered on what is most important for you to be involved in. While you should be open to the various ways in which God may direct you to help others, you must not become sidetracked by a myriad of needs, because there will always be more needs than you can personally handle.

Being Perplexed over Multiple Talents

Some people never pursue their true visions because they have the "problem" of being multi-talented, of being able to do many things. A misunderstanding of their gifts causes many talented and intelligent people to be ineffective and unsuccessful in life. These people say, "I have so many gifts that I don't know which ones I'm supposed to use. I want to develop all of them." As a result, they develop none of them to proficiency. I have many interests myself. I'm a teacher, a preacher, a speaker, and a writer. I can also paint, sculpt, and write and play music. However, I have had to focus on specific gifts in order to be effective in life.

Let me ask you this: Have you ever seen anyone who became successful in life by doing everything? Think about people such as Helen Keller, Picasso, Marie Curie, Tiger Woods, tennis champions Serena and Venus Williams, Bill Gates, and Mother Theresa. Each of these people did one or two things very well, and it became the source of their life and their prosperity. It made room for them in the world.

When a person tries to do everything, he ends up becoming a "jack-of-all-trades and master of none." I'm sure you know some multi-gifted people who seem to have the best chances of success but who aren't doing anything with their lives. You have to guard against the temptation to try to do everything. No matter how many gifts you have, don't let them distract you. You must decide to concentrate on one or two gifts, and then stir them up. Don't worry about losing the other gifts. Decide which gift you are going to stir up; as you stir that one up, the other gifts will follow it. God will not waste what He has given you.

Not Recognizing the Cost of Vision

The second obstacle to fulfilling vision is not recognizing the cost of accomplishing it. I think many people believe that successful people are born successful. In reality, success comes in installments, similar to a payment plan. It's a process, and I'll talk more about that process later in this book. You receive a little bit of success today, a little more tomorrow, and more next week.

One of the costs of vision is diligence. All human beings dream, yet only the few who wake up, get out of their beds of comfort, and work hard will experience the fulfillment of their dreams. Often, what causes us not to recognize and pay the cost of vision is the feeling that our lives are out of our own control and that there's nothing we can do to change that.

Blaming "Bad Luck"

For example, if you think you have had a string of bad luck in life or that you are an unlucky person, you will probably not make the effort necessary to make your vision succeed. You may think, "Why bother?" This type of reasoning can undermine your entire life, destroying your desire to achieve your goals. You must realize that **you are not defined by your past or confined by external factors.**

Blaming Outside Forces

Some people believe that others are responsible for causing their visions to fail. Maybe their parents couldn't afford to send them to college, and now they are bitter and resentful because they didn't pursue the careers they wanted to. Maybe they had children sooner than they expected, and this caused them to feel they had to give up their dreams. **Life will present us with challenges, but this fact doesn't have to derail our visions.** If you want something badly enough, you will be patient in acquiring it, even if the timetable isn't what you would have wanted. Don't allow yourself to feel that you are a victim of the actions or needs of others.

Success comes in installments.

There are people who think that their past experiences—educational, social, spiritual—or their past failures preclude them from having a vision for their lives. Please realize this: God is not against you. He is for you. Do you believe that in your heart? He still has a definite plan and purpose for your life in spite of your background or your mistakes. No matter what you've done, God is not finished until He's completed what He created you to be and do.

We often imagine that our pasts loom larger than our futures. Sometimes, we think that what we have done is so bad that it is greater than Jesus' sacrifice for us on the cross. Yet nothing is so bad that it can compete with the forgiveness of Jesus. If you have had a baby out of wedlock, if you have been on drugs, if you have been to prison, if you have betrayed someone, God still loves you and wants to redeem you. He wants to give you back your purpose.

The Bible says, *"Every good and perfect gift is from above, coming down from the Father of the heavenly lights, who does not change like shifting shadows"* (James 1:17). This is a very important statement about God. It says that God gives gifts, and that when He gives a gift, He doesn't change His mind regarding it. Whatever God has invested in you, He wants to see used. He is a good God who gives good gifts to all people, and He doesn't vary or change in this expectation.

Your purpose is greater than your failures and mistakes.

Don't ever believe that your failures are greater than what God gave you birth to do. God is a restorer, a reclaimer. This means He will put back in you what the world took out. He'll put back in you what life took out. Ask Him to restore His purpose and vision within you.

Let me urge you not to allow circumstances to destroy your passion for living. Don't allow life to blow you from one side of the lake to the other. The winds of adversity can be very strong, but your God-given vision will be your anchor in life.

Not Knowing the Principles for Fulfilling Vision

The third obstacle to accomplishing vision is not knowing the principles for fulfilling it. Successful visionaries don't pursue their visions haphazardly; instead, they operate according to established and time-tested principles that enable their visions to become reality. In Part II of this book, I have outlined "Twelve Principles for Fulfilling Personal Vision." In this section, I give you positive ways to pursue your vision as you actively put the principles into practice.

Let Your Life Be Fueled by Vision

Life was designed to be inspired by purpose and fueled by vision. This means that you don't have to live a defensive life that is made up of crisis management; instead, you can pursue an offensive life that steadily follows its vision and initiates its own goals and actions. The following pages will help you to clarify your vision, formulate a plan for accomplishing it, and bring it to a fulfilling and successful completion.

Action Steps to Fulfilling Vision

- What do you think is your greatest obstacle to pursuing and completing your vision?

- What steps can you take to begin overcoming that obstacle? (For example, have you distinguished between your life's mission and its vision? Will you trust that your life is under God's purposes and that you are not a victim of "bad luck"? Will you stop blaming others for the way your life has turned out and start thanking God that He will enable you to complete His vision for your life?)

Chapter Principles

1. Three major obstacles to fulfilling vision are (1) not under-
    standing the nature of vision, (2) not recognizing the cost of
    vision, and (3) not knowing the principles of vision.

2. The essential nature of vision is that it is specific.

3. Mission is a general statement of purpose while vision is
    a very precise statement with a specific emphasis and defin-
    able boundaries.

4. The measure of the success of your vision is God's assign-
    ment to you, not what others are doing.

5. Dreaming is only the beginning of vision. Instead of wish-
    ing things would get better, we must take concrete steps to
    change our lives.

6. Indecisiveness is a vision-killer and drains the joy out of life.

7. If you set a destination for your life while you continue to pray
    about your vision, God will guide you where you need to go.

8. You were not born or created to do everything. You were
    meant to meet certain needs, not every need.

9. When you have several gifts and talents, focus on one or two
    of them and stir them up. Don't allow multiple gifts to distract
    you from taking specific steps toward fulfilling your vision.

10. You are not defined by your past or confined by external fac-
    tors.

11. God has a definite plan and purpose for your life in spite of
    what your background is or what mistakes you have made.

12. When God gives a gift to someone, He doesn't change His
    mind about it. Whatever God has invested in you, He wants
    to see used.

Part II

Twelve Principles for Fulfilling Personal Vision

Introduction to Part II

Jeremiah 29:11 tells us, *"'I know the plans I have for you,' declares the LORD, 'plans to prosper you and not to harm you, plans to give you hope and a future.'"* God has plans for us, and He wants those plans to be fulfilled. Yet for this to happen, we must follow His direction. In the first chapter of the book of Joshua, God established the key to fulfilling His plans. This is the background to the passage: Moses had died, and Joshua was set to take over leadership of the Israelites in order to bring them into the Promised Land. God said to Joshua, in effect, "Moses is now dead, but you have a big vision; it's your time now to fulfill your purpose. Let's see what you're going to do." The Lord's first advice to Joshua was to be sure to obey His Word:

> *Be strong and very courageous. Be careful to obey all the law my servant Moses gave you; do not turn from it to the right or to the left, that you may be successful wherever you go. Do not let this Book of the Law depart from your mouth; meditate on it day and night, so that you may be careful to do every-thing written in it. Then you will be prosperous and successful* ["have good success" NKJV]. (Joshua 1:7–8)

In other words, God was saying to Joshua, "You will be successful if you learn and follow My precepts and principles." God guaranteed him success if he would obey the commands that Moses himself had had to obey. Note that God didn't tell Joshua to literally imitate Moses' *life*, but to follow Moses' *principles*, the ones Moses had used in his own work. Likewise, you can never—nor should you ever—imitate someone else's life.

However, you can and should follow the established principles of successful visionaries. The "Twelve Principles for Fulfilling Personal Vision" that follow have been used by people of vision and are designed to protect, preserve, and guarantee the fulfillment of your dream. If you can capture these principles, you will move beyond survival mode; you will be an overcomer and see your vision come to pass.

God has never created a failure. He designed you, sculpted you, and gave you birth to be a success. If you have failed, it is only because you are a success who went off track. Remember that you don't have to stay on the sidelines. Redemption restores to you the ability to accomplish your vision.

Anyone can be successful. I have seen personally how God enables people to transform ideas into a reality that can be seen in the physical world. The problem is that few people are following the principles that lead to success. Either they don't know the principles, or they have never proven them by putting them into practice. These people don't allow the principles of vision to work in their lives and, consequently, they don't experience the fulfillment of their visions. A successful person is someone who understands, submits to, and adheres to the principles that will carry him to success.

The "Twelve Principles for Fulfilling Personal Vision" will help you find your target and stay on course. These principles are neither personal nor private. They may be clearly discerned from the Scriptures and the lives of accomplished visionaries, and they are historically proven. Jesus Himself had to use each one of these principles to be successful in His work of redemption. You cannot avoid them or ignore them. If you don't go through them, you will have little chance of achieving your life's vision. If you are careful to put them into practice, however, you will have good success.

Chapter Four

Principle #1:
Be Directed by a
Clear Vision

To FULFILL YOUR VISION, YOU MUST HAVE A CLEAR
GUIDING PURPOSE FOR YOUR LIFE.

The first principle of vision is that you must have a clear guiding purpose for your life. Every effective leader or group of people in history has had one thing in common: They were directed by a clear vision. Remember that Moses, Joshua, David, and Nehemiah each had visions that drove them and motivated their actions. The first thing God gave to Abraham was a specific vision. He showed him the Promised Land and said, "That's your vision. You're going to take your offspring there."

I cannot stress enough the need for a guiding vision in life because it is perhaps the single most important key to fulfilling your dream. You personally, as an individual, must have your own guiding life vision. This vision must be *absolutely clear* to you because, otherwise, you will have nothing to aim at, and you will achieve nothing.

As I wrote earlier, when you know and understand what you were born to accomplish, that is purpose. When you can see it in your mind by faith and begin to imagine it, that is vision.

You cannot contribute to God's greater purpose if you don't know your personal vision. If you have no sense of focus, you will just drift along. I like what Jesus said in Luke 2:49: *"I must be about my Father's business"* (KJV). There were many other businesses Jesus could have been about, but He identified a specific life work that was His own and that motivated everything He did.

A clear guiding purpose will keep you from being distracted by nonessentials.

Whether you are young, middle-aged, or older, if you don't have a clear purpose, you are going to be distracted by every other business in the world, because the world is an extremely busy place. You must realize that when you set your mind on what you want to do, all the other business of the world will try to get in the way of it. Having a clear guiding purpose will enable you to stay on track when you are tempted to be distracted by lesser or nonessential things.

The What and the Why of Existence

One of my undergraduate degrees is in education, and I had to take a course in biology for a full year as part of my degree requirements. I really enjoyed that course because it was extremely detailed. We studied the neurological and circulatory systems of the human body, the bone structure, the brain cells, and all the intricacies of how the body works. At the end of the class, I received an A. I was very proud of myself. Yet while I was looking at my grade, boasting to myself about what a good job I had done and how much I had learned about the human body, a question burst into my mind: "Now that you know *what* the human body is, do you know *why* it is"? Education can give us knowledge, but it can't always give us reasons.

I discovered then that the key to life is not only knowing what you are, but also why you are. **It is more important to know why you were born than to know the fact that you were born.**

If you don't know your reason for existence, you will begin to experiment with your life, and that is dangerous. You must capture a meaning for your life, a clear vision for your existence. You should know who you are—that is, your origin and purpose in God—as well as your abilities and plans for the future.

When you decide on a vision, don't sell yourself short.

Let me ask you some difficult but necessary questions: Have you changed jobs several times in the last few years? Do you keep changing your major in college? Do you do one thing for a time and then go on to something else because you are bored or dissatisfied? If so, you lack vision. You were not created to be bored and dissatisfied. For the last thirty years, I have been praying that God would give me an extra day in the week so I can do more work toward my vision. I can't wait to get up in the morning, and I don't like to see the sun go down. Why? I want to squeeze everything I can out of each day because I have a vision that keeps me passionate. Proverbs 6:10–11 says, *"A little sleep, a little slumber, a little folding of the hands to rest—and poverty will come on you like a bandit and scarcity like an armed man."* Lazy people are visionless people. Bored people are those who haven't yet found their purpose.

You *must* choose where you want to go in life and then be decisive and faithful in carrying it out. Don't put off the decision or be afraid of it. Moreover, when you're deciding, make sure not to sell yourself short. Shooting for the clouds is too low. Instead, make the clouds your cushion in case you fall.

Remember that a vision is not the same thing as a goal, such as building a house, buying a sports car, or having a million dollars in the bank. Having a purpose and vision has to do with your life existence. It enables you to answer the question, "Why was I born?" While you can't know all the ramifications of your life, which God may reveal to you in eternity, you should have a good idea of the purpose He has given you to accomplish on earth. Without it, all you're doing is existing.

A Job versus a Vision

I want to illustrate for you the difference between simply having a job and having a clear guiding purpose by looking at the life of Nehemiah. Nehemiah had a job as the cupbearer to Artaxerxes, the king of Persia (Nehemiah 1:11). This seems to have been an important position that may have included both serving wine to the king and his royal guests and tasting the king's wine to make sure it wasn't poisoned. Yet being a cupbearer meant much more than this. Nehemiah was in a top position in the king's court and was a highly regarded, trusted, and influential advisor to the king.*

As prestigious as Nehemiah's occupation was, it was simply a job for him because his mind was occupied with something else. Nehemiah was a descendant of one of the large number of Jews who had been carried into captivity by the Babylonians. The Babylonians were subsequently defeated by the Persians, and that is why Nehemiah was serving a Persian king.

At the time of the Babylonian captivity, the city of Jerusalem had undergone terrible destruction. Yet, when the Babylonians were defeated seventy years later, fifty thousand Jews had returned to Judea and had rebuilt the temple. Then, an effort to rebuild the walls of Jerusalem was thwarted by opposition from neighboring peoples who had convinced King Artaxerxes to issue a decree to stop the work. In the first chapter of the book of Nehemiah, Nehemiah heard that *"the wall of Jerusalem is broken down, and its gates have been burned with fire"* (v. 3). Some believe this destruction refers to the original devastation of Jerusalem, while others think it is a reference to this particular opposition to rebuilding the wall.‡

---

* See R. Laird Harris, "Nehemiah," in *The New International Dictionary of the Bible*, J. D. Douglas and Merrill C. Tenney, eds. (Grand Rapids, MI: Zondervan Publishing House, 1987), 699; and *The Wesley Bible: A Personal Study Bible for Holy Living*, Albert F. Harper, gen. ed. (Nashville: Thomas Nelson Publishers, 1990), 669.

‡ See *The Wycliffe Bible Commentary*, Charles F. Pfeiffer and Everett F. Harrison, eds. (Chicago: Moody Press, 1962), 427, 435–36.

Either way, the news filled Nehemiah with grief. When he heard that the wall of Jerusalem was broken down and that everything was in disarray, he *"sat down and wept. For some days* [he] *mourned and fasted and prayed before the God of heaven"* (Nehemiah 1:4).

Your True Work Is What You Were Born to Do

I like to think of Nehemiah's cupbearer job as his preliminary occupation, or his "pre-occupation," because he was born to fulfill another, much more important role. Your true work is what you were born to do. Your job is what you do only until you are ready to fulfill your vision. God had placed in Nehemiah's heart a vision of rebuilding the wall: *"I had not* [yet] *told anyone what my God had put in my heart to do for Jerusalem"* (Nehemiah 2:12).

Your vision will bother you until you take action on it.

Nehemiah 2:1 reads, *"In the month of Nisan in the twentieth year of King Artaxerxes, when wine was brought for him, I took the wine and gave it to the king. I had not been sad in his presence before."* The implication here is that Nehemiah was doing fine on his job until he heard about the wall. Then he had the idea to rebuild it. He went to God in prayer about it, and God told him to go back and reconstruct it. This was the compelling vision of Nehemiah's life. His desire to accomplish his life's work then began to interfere with his job. He was employed by the king, but his yearning to rebuild the wall began to wear on him, and he became depressed. The king said to him, *"Why does your face look so sad when you are not ill? This can be nothing but sadness of heart"* (v. 2).

When God gives you a vision and confirms it, nothing can stop it. If He tells you to build, start, invest, create, or manufacture something, then it will bother you deep inside; you will become depressed until you do it. This is a "sanctified" depression, however, the kind that says, "I won't be satisfied until I complete my vision."

Is your true work—your purpose—making it uncomfortable for you to stay in your present job? That was Nehemiah's situation. He was continually troubled until he was able to take action on his vision. People who know what they are called to do seem to be possessed by their visions. In a sense, they are. They are possessed by the things God has given them to accomplish. Nehemiah saw the wall completed in his mind's eye before he started to work on it, and that vision drove his passion.

What Do You Want?

When the king saw Nehemiah's sadness, he asked him one of the most significant questions anyone can ask a person: *"What is it you want?"* (Nehemiah 2:4). What is equally significant is that Nehemiah was able to answer it specifically. He said, *"Let* [the king] *send me to the city in Judah where my fathers are buried so that I can rebuild it"* (v. 5). Nehemiah knew his clear guiding vision, and his plan was so specific that he was able to give the king a time frame for completing it. **You need to seriously ask yourself the same question: "What is it that I want?"**

Do you know what you really want out of life? Some people just want to indulge in self-serving activities. Others think life begins at retirement, and they miss out on practically their entire lives. Some people just want to own a house. Yet once they get their house, then what? They want to buy a nicer car. Fine. Then what? They want children. Yet once they have children, then what? There has to be something more to life than the things we accumulate. In Luke 12:15, Jesus said, *"A man's life does not consist in the abundance of his possessions."* Your true vision is not a house or car or even children, since sometimes we treat our children as possessions. There is something more important in life than the "trophies" we like to gather around ourselves. In order to find your vision, you must be in touch with the values and priorities of the kingdom of God. **Your vision should be something that lives on after you're gone, something that has greater lasting**

power than possessions. People's lives should be changed by your vision. What do you want? The King of Kings is asking you this question today, and you must be able to give Him an answer.

Vision is a clear conception of something that is not yet reality, but which can exist.

How do you answer His question? First, you ask Him to confirm what He has put in your heart for you to do. Nehemiah's first response to the problem in Jerusalem was, "Let me go to God in prayer." He had a passion for God and His ways, and he cried out to God to give him clear direction about what he should do. He had a burning passion within him to address the problems of his people. Perhaps you know what this burning is like. You feel frustrated about certain things you see in your neighborhood and your country. You have a strong desire to see change, and you have prayed, "God, something's wrong with our country, something's wrong with our neighborhoods, something's wrong with our marriages." Nehemiah went to God, and God heard his prayer and answered it by confirming what he should do. Your vision uniquely belongs to you as a person called by God. As you pray, it will become clear to you.

Vision Is a Preferable Future

Your vision is a clear conception of something that is not yet reality, but which can exist. It is a strong image of a preferable future. This means that the present is not enough; something else is needed. You should never settle for what you currently have. In fact, a true visionary irritates those who want things to remain as they always have. Vision is always pushing the envelope. It demands change by its very nature.

This is a very important point. Because of the fact that vision is often clarified through the desire to solve a problem, as in Nehemiah's case, many people don't realize that vision is active *even when times are good and things are in a positive state.*

87

Why will God activate a vision when things are going well? To stir up your life so that you will move forward and progress rather than becoming complacent. When everything is going along as it always has been, and you are getting used to your situation, you may forget about your vision. God may then use a vision to shake you out of your indifference. A vision will always take you from good to better and from better to best.

Vision is always future-focused. Sometimes, people say, "Let's go back to the good old days." Yet if we do that, we will not progress in what God has planned for us. We need to *build on* the past, but we cannot return to it.

I confess that the temptation to focus on the "good old days" has been one of my challenges in life. Vision does not mean regaining what you had; it means moving forward to gain what you have never had. Vision doesn't try to recapture the good old days; rather, it desires to create days that have not yet existed. If you're going to pursue vision, you have to be careful how you use tradition and memories of good things. Sometimes, memories can prevent you from seeing miracles because they keep you stuck in the past. God wants to do great works in our lives, and we have to be careful not to miss these opportunities by a false view of what has come before.

When you are very close to a visionary, or very close to a vision, you're constantly going to be driven to change. To go to a new place, you have to go to a new location. You also have to think in a new way. That sometimes causes discomfort. Vision can constantly keep you unsettled, but it also keeps you fluid and mobile, ready to take the next step toward your vision. This truth is essential to understand because, when you keep company with God, you have to keep moving. When the Israelites were traveling in the desert, they would put down their stakes and set up their tents, but soon the pillar of cloud would move again, and they would need to follow it. God keeps us going so we don't become stagnant. **A clear vision gives us a passion that keeps us continually moving forward in life.**

Action Steps to Fulfilling Vision

- Have you truly answered the King's question, "What is it that you want in life?" Write down your answer.

- What things in your life are distracting you from the real "business" of your life?

Chapter Principles

1. You must have a clear guiding purpose for your life.

2. The key to life is not only knowing what you are, but also *why* you are.

3. Your true work is what you were born to do. Your job is what you are doing just until you are ready to fulfill your vision.

4. When God gives you a vision, it will bother you until you do it.

5. One of the most significant questions we must each answer for ourselves is *"What is it you want?"* (Nehemiah 2:4).

6. Your vision should be something that lives on after you're gone.

7. Your vision is a clear conception of something that is not yet reality, but which can exist. It is a strong image of a preferable future.

8. A vision demands change by its very nature.

9. A vision is active even when times are good and things are in a positive state.

10. Vision doesn't try to recapture the good old days; rather, it desires to create days that have not yet existed.

11. When you keep company with God, you have to keep moving.

12. A clear vision gives us a passion that keeps us continually moving forward in life.

Chapter Five
Principle #2:
Know Your Potential for Fulfilling Vision

WHEN YOU DISCOVER YOUR DREAM, YOU WILL ALSO DISCOVER YOUR
ABILITY TO FULFILL IT.

Second, you will never be successful in your vision until you truly understand your potential. Recall that your potential is determined by the assignment God has given you to do. **Whatever you were *born* to do, you are *equipped* to do.** Moreover, resources will become available to you as you need them.

What this means is that God gives ability to fulfill responsibility. Therefore, when you discover your dream, you will also discover your ability. God will never call you to an assignment without giving you the provision for accomplishing it. If you understand this principle, no one can stop you from fulfilling your vision.

We must come into an awareness of our potential. Potential is hidden capacity, untapped power, unreleased energy. It is all you could be but haven't yet become. Potential is who you really are, in accordance with your vision, even if you don't yet know your true self. Potential is the person who has been trapped inside you because of false ideas of who you are—either your own or others'. God has created you to do something wonderful, and He has given you the ability and resources you need to do it.

The Power at Work within Us

Ephesians 3:20 says, *"Now to him who is able to do immeasurably* [*"exceeding abundantly"* KJV] *more than all we ask or imagine, according to his power that is at work within us."* Many of us have heard this verse so many times that we think we know it. Yet I don't believe we really understand what it is saying: *"According to his power* [or potential] *that is at work"*—where? It doesn't say His power is at work in heaven. It says it is at work in us! God put His vision and His Spirit within us, and that is more than enough potential for our needs.

Your imagination isn't big enough for all God wants to do for you.

What are the implications of this truth? It means that what you are able to accomplish has nothing to do with who your parents were. It has nothing to do with your past or with physical factors such as your race or appearance. Instead, it has to do with *"the power"* working within you. That power is the mighty power of God's Spirit who lives inside you, enabling you to fulfill the vision He has given you. God's power is actually working within you for the fulfillment of your dream.

This Scripture changed my life at a point when I wasn't manifesting much of my purpose. I was brought up with the religious idea that you receive only what you ask for. Consequently, I didn't receive much. Then I came to understand that God never promised to give me merely what I asked for. Instead, He said something truly extraordinary: He will do *"immeasurably"* or *"exceeding abundantly"* beyond all that I can ask for, think about, or imagine. In other words, my imagination is not big enough for all that He wants to do for me.

Once I grasped this truth, it began to transform my perspective. It enabled me to progress from the knowledge of my purpose to the faith that accompanies vision. For example, in my mind's eye, I have already been in the buildings that will be built for Bahamas Faith Ministries in accordance with the vision God has given me. In my imagination, I've gone up in the elevator to the seventh floor of the hotel. I've been in the boardroom talking with leaders from around the world who are gathered there. I have visited the convention center. I believe God will bring this vision to pass. And that is only what *I* can imagine. God has even more in His own imagination for the completion of this vision!

Take a Tour of Your Dream

We can't begin to imagine all the things God wants to do for us. **Yet God gave us the gift of imagination to keep us from focusing only on our present conditions.** He wants us to take a "tour" of our visions on a regular basis.

What do you imagine doing? Go on a tour of your dream. Visit everything. Check it out. See all the details. Notice its value. Then come back to the present and say, "Let's go there, God!"

God told Jeremiah, *"Before I formed you in the womb I knew you, before you were born I set you apart; I appointed you as a prophet to the nations"* (Jeremiah 1:5). Notice that God used the past tense. He had already set apart and appointed Jeremiah as a prophet. Yet at first, Jeremiah responded, *"I do not know how to speak"* (v. 6). God's reaction was, in effect, "Do not say that! If I built you to be a prophet, don't tell Me you can't talk!" (See verses 6–7.)

Once God showed Jeremiah why he was born, Jeremiah discovered what he could do. In other words, when Jeremiah understood his vision, he began to realize his ability. At first he didn't think he could speak publicly for God. Whatever God calls for, however, He provides for. Whatever He requires, He enables us to do. In this case, God gave Jeremiah the ability to

93

speak for Him: *"Then the* LORD *reached out his hand and touched my mouth and said to me, 'Now I have put my words in your mouth'"* (Jeremiah 1:9).

You must understand that God will never call you to do something that He hasn't already given you the ability to do or that He won't give you the ability to do when the time comes. **You shouldn't allow any other human being to judge your potential.** Others may not be able to see your purpose, and your abilities are determined by your purpose. Again, whatever God is causing you to dream is a revelation of your ability. Responsibility is really "respond-ability" or the ability to respond to the requirements of your vision.

You Are Perfect for Your Purpose

Everything about you is determined by your purpose. God built you, designed you, and gave you the right makeup for it. Your heritage and ethnic mix, the color of your skin, your language, your height, and all your other physical features are made for the fulfillment of your vision. You were built for what you're supposed to do. You are perfect for your purpose.

Dreams are given to draw out what's already inside us and to activate God's power.

This means that your ability isn't dependent on what you perceive as your limitations. How many people have made statements such as these: "I don't have enough education"; "I'm too ugly"; "I'm too short"; "I'm part of a minority group"? They have a long list of reasons why they can't do what they are dreaming. None of those excuses are valid. Everything God gave you to do, you are able to do. For everything God put in your heart to do, you have the corresponding ability to accomplish.

Dreams are given to draw out what's already inside us and to activate God's power in enabling us to achieve our visions. This is why God may give us dreams that are bigger than our educations. For instance, I shouldn't be able to do what I am currently doing, based on my background and the expectations of the society I grew up in. Likewise, you may not have the background to do what you are going to do. People may not believe you can do it, yet what does it matter what they think? Just keep doing what God tells you to do.

Your present job may contain hidden potential for your true life's work.

God never gives us dreams to frustrate us. He gives us dreams to deliver us from mediocrity and to reveal our true selves to the world. The more I study the Word of God, the more I realize that God appoints, anoints, and distinguishes people. He doesn't like them to get lost in mediocrity. Therefore, He said, in effect, "Abraham, come out. Moses, come out. David, come out. You are lost among the average."

Potential Is Realized When You Say Yes to Your Dream

The ability to accomplish your vision is manifested when you say yes to your dream and obey God. Nehemiah's job of cupbearer, in itself, did not give him the ability to rebuild the wall of Jerusalem. If he had looked only at the resources he had at that time, he never would have fulfilled his vision. Yet God had placed him in his position for a reason, and Nehemiah trusted God to provide what was needed. You don't know how your present job may contain hidden potential for your true life's work. It may make a way for the resources you will need to fulfill your vision. Nehemiah had favor as a trusted servant of the monarch, and God gave him even more favor with the king so that he could fulfill his vision. God reveals our potential as we act on our dreams.

Note that after Nehemiah had stepped out in faith and articulated his vision in answer to the king's question, *"What is it you want?"* (Nehemiah 2:4), his ability and resources came into place. The king gave Nehemiah letters granting him safe passage to Jerusalem and giving him access to timber from the king's forest for the rebuilding of the wall. The king basically paid for the project. Moreover, the king appointed Nehemiah as governor in the land of Judah so that he had the authority to carry out the reconstruction of the wall. (See Nehemiah 2:7–10; 5:14.)

You can always determine what you can do by the dream that is within you.

To better understand this truth, let's consider an analogy from nature. In Creation, God gave trees the ability to reproduce themselves through their seed. By doing this, He was commanding trees to come out of seeds. First He put the potential for the trees in the seeds. Then He told humankind, in essence, "If you plant the seeds, putting them in the right environment, they will eventually become what I put in them—their potential—fully grown trees."

Our lives are like seed. We were born with the potential for the fulfillment of our destinies that have already been established within us. When God gives a vision to someone, He's simply calling forth what He put into that person. This is why you can always determine what you can do by the dream that is within you. **Plant the seed of your vision by beginning to act on it and then nurture it by faith.** Your vision will develop until it is fully grown and bears much fruit in the world.

Action Steps to Fulfilling Vision
- Take a "virtual tour" of your dream. Imagine all the details of the completed vision. Then let God know that is where you want to go. Ask Him to enable you to take your idea from dream to full-fledged reality.

- How can you begin to "plant the seed" of your vision today?

Chapter Principles

1. You will never be successful in your vision until you truly understand your potential.

2. Your potential is determined by the assignment God gave you to do. Whatever you were born to do, you are equipped to do.

3. God gives ability to fulfill responsibility. When you discover your dream, you will also discover your ability.

4. Our power or potential is at work in us. God put His vision and His Spirit within us, and that is more than enough potential for our needs.

5. God will do *"immeasurably"* or *"exceeding abundantly"* beyond all that we can ask for, think about, or imagine. Our imaginations are not big enough for all that He wants to do for us.

6. God gave us the gift of imagination to keep us from focusing only on our present conditions.

7. Whatever God calls for, He provides for. Whatever He requires, He enables us to do.

8. Your ability isn't dependent on what you perceive as your limitations. You are perfect for your purpose.

9. Dreams are given to us to draw out what's already inside us and to activate God's power in enabling us to achieve our visions.

10. God appoints, anoints, and distinguishes people. He doesn't like them to get lost in mediocrity. God gives us dreams to deliver us from mediocrity and to reveal our true selves to the world.

11. The ability to accomplish your vision is manifested when you say yes to your dream and obey God.

Chapter Six
Principle #3: Develop a Concrete Plan for Your Vision

TO MAN BELONG THE PLANS OF THE HEART.
—PROVERBS 16:1

T hird, to be successful, you must have a clear plan. There is no future without planning. I've known people who tried to be successful over and over again without a plan. It never works.

God Gives the Vision, and We Make the Plans

When I was a teenager and had been a Christian for only about two years, I kept wondering why God didn't seem to be guiding me in my life. Perhaps you are wondering the same thing about your own life. I used to want God to show me His will at night in my room, so I would stay up all night with one eye open, just waiting. I used to pray, "Oh, Lord, let the angels show up." Then I would look and there would be nothing but mosquitoes. Sometimes, I would hear a little noise outside and I would open the door, thinking that the angels had shown up. Yet when I looked outside, all I would see was a rat running across the yard. Some angel!

I persisted in wanting God to show Himself to me and to guide me. Whenever they sang a certain song in church, I used to sing it the loudest: "Lead me, guide me, along the way!" One day, as I was singing this song, I felt as if the Lord was saying to me, "Lead you along *what* way?" I realized then that if you don't have a plan, God doesn't have anything specific to direct you in.

Proverbs 16:1 says, *"To man belong the plans of the heart, but from the LORD comes the reply of the tongue."* That's a very powerful statement. God is saying, in effect, "I gave you the vision. Now you put the plan on paper, and I will work out the details." Proverbs 16:9 says, *"In his heart a man plans his course, but the LORD determines his steps."* If you don't have a plan, how can He direct you?

God will direct your steps once you make a plan to move toward what you desire.

Have you expressed to God what is in your heart, and have you presented Him with your plan for accomplishing it? The Bible says that God will give you the desires of your heart if you will delight in Him (Psalm 37:4). However, it also implies that God will direct your steps once you make a concrete plan to move toward what you desire.

Ideas are seeds of destiny planted by God in the minds of humankind. **When ideas are cultivated, they become imagination. Imagination, if it is watered and developed, becomes a plan. Finally, if a plan is followed, it becomes a reality.** However, when a person receives an idea from God, it must be cultivated soon or the idea often goes away. If that person doesn't ever work on the idea, God will give it to someone else. Inevitably, if the second person takes the idea, makes a plan, and starts to work on it, the first person will become jealous because he had the idea first! Yet it's not just having ideas that is important. Ideas need plans if they are going to become reality.

Young people often think their dreams will just happen. They find out later, after they have sadly wasted many years of their lives, that this is not the case. There is no way any of us can move toward our dreams without a plan. Jesus said that a wise person doesn't start to build something unless he first works out the details:

> *Suppose one of you wants to build a tower. Will he not first sit down and estimate the cost to see if he has enough money to complete it? For if he lays the foundation and is not able to finish it, everyone who sees it will ridicule him, saying, "This fellow began to build and was not able to finish."* (Luke 14:28–30)

God Himself had a plan when He created humanity. Ephesians 1:11 says, *"In him we were also chosen, having been predestined according to the plan of him who works out everything in conformity with the purpose of his will."*

Someone once said to me, "You always seem to be going somewhere. Just relax." I told him, "I've discovered something about life. Where I live in the Bahamas, when you just sit on a boat in the ocean and relax, the current takes you wherever it's going, even if you don't want to go there. Life is the same way." Too many people float down their lives and still expect to make it to their goals.

When you lack a plan, you miss opportunities.

A ship has a compass so that the navigator can know what direction he is going in, and it has a rudder so that the pilot can steer it. However, a ship is given a specific course—a plan—by the captain, so that it can arrive at its destination. All three are necessary—the compass, the rudder, and the plan. Just because a ship has a rudder doesn't necessarily mean it is going anywhere. It needs to be steered according to the coordinates of the plan. Likewise, life has given many people clear sailing, yet, because they have no destination, they never make it out of port. What do I mean by clear sailing? I mean opportunities. Many opportunities come to people, but they have no plan in place that would enable them to make something out of them.

For example, suppose you wish you could start a business, but you've never thought about how you'd go about it. What if someone came to you and said, "I want to invest some money, and I like you. Why don't you develop something with it?" You would probably answer something like, "I'd like to, but right now I'm just a clerk...." However, if you had developed a specific plan, if you were reading the appropriate books and preparing yourself, if you had everything down on paper, you'd be prepared for this opportunity. You could say, "You have the money? Here's the plan. I'm ready to go!"

The Blueprint of Your Vision

When a contractor is building a structure, he uses a blueprint. That is his plan for his vision, which is the finished building. The contractor always keeps a copy of his blueprint on site with him. Why? He needs to keep checking it to see if the building is being constructed correctly. If you don't have a plan for your life, you have nothing to refer to when you want to make sure you are on track. How do you begin developing a blueprint for your vision?

Who Am I?

Again, you must first secure for yourself the answer to the question "Who am I?" Until you do, it will be difficult to write a plan for your life because such a plan is directly tied to knowing who you are. You will never become really successful in your life if you don't have a clear idea of your own identity in God. Many of us have become what other people want us to be. We have not yet discovered our unique, irreplaceable identity. Yet it is knowing your true identity that gives you the courage to write your life plan.

Where Am I Going?

Next, you must answer the question "Where am I going?" Once you learn God's purpose, you can start planning effectively because you will be able to plan with focus. **A vision becomes a plan when it is captured, fleshed out, and written down.**

Please note that both verses one and nine of Proverbs 16 say that God leaves the planning up to the heart of the person, but that He will provide the explanation as to how the vision will be accomplished. The plan that's in your heart is a documentation of a future that is not yet finished. When you write down a plan, it's a description of the end of your life, not the beginning. That is why God says, "You make the plan, and I will explain how it can be paid for, who is going to work with it, and where the resources and facilities are going to come from. Leave that part to Me. You just put the plans down."

Do you have a plan for the next fifty years of your life?

I'm a stickler for planning. Anyone who works with me will tell you that. I have plans for what I'm going to do next week, next month, next year, and five years from now. In fact, the vision for Bahamas Faith Ministries is on paper for the next sixty or seventy years. It's all mapped out. By then, I'll be about 110 years old, walking around, looking at the buildings, and saying, "Hey, look at that! Look at all the students over there. I remember when we had one building. Now we have ten buildings. Glory to God!"

Do you have a plan? Do you know what you want to do next week, next month, next year, five years from now? Do you have a plan for the next twenty years of your life? Can you give me a plan for your life for the next fifty years? God has given you the ability to do that. He has given you a mind, the gift of imagination, the anointing of the Holy Spirit, and the vision of faith. He has also given you the ability to write so that you can put down what you see in your heart. What are you waiting for? God says He will explain how your vision will be accomplished, yet He can't discuss it with you until you have something concrete to talk about.

Your Dream Is Worth Writing Down

Note the way Nehemiah planned for his vision of rebuilding the wall of Jerusalem:

103

I went to Jerusalem, and after staying there three days I set out during the night with a few men. I had not told anyone what my God had put in my heart to do for Jerusalem. There were no mounts with me except the one I was riding on. By night I went out through the Valley Gate toward the Jackal Well and the Dung Gate, examining the walls of Jerusalem, which had been broken down, and its gates, which had been destroyed by fire....I went up the valley by night, examining the wall. Finally, I turned back and reentered through the Valley Gate. The officials did not know where I had gone or what I was doing, because as yet I had said nothing to the Jews or the priests or nobles or officials or any others who would be doing the work. (Nehemiah 2:11–13, 15–16)

Nehemiah did not take action until he had made a plan. He selected only a few trusted men to go with him while he was assessing the situation because not everyone could have handled the plan at that point. Certain people can't handle your plan while you're making it. That is why you can't tell it to everyone. Sometimes, you have to write it in private and keep it secret for a time. Some people will try to talk you out of your plan, saying, "You can't do that!" If you listen to them, in no time, you will throw your plan away and end up an average person, like they are. People who are going nowhere like to take others with them. Those who aren't doing anything want other people to do it with them.

Not everybody will understand what you're dreaming, but put your dream on paper anyway. Why? *Your dream is worth writing down.* If God gave it to you, it deserves to be done. For example, if you want to go to college to pursue a certain career, write down your plans for the next ten years. Entitle one of the pages in your plan, "This is what I want to be ten years from now." Whatever you want to establish or achieve, put it on paper and say, "By the year _____, this is where I want to be."

Start with What You Have

After Nehemiah had made his plan, he was ready to talk to others about it. He talked to those who would be directly involved in carrying it out. *"Then I said to* [the Jews, priests, nobles, officials, and others], *'You see the trouble we are in: Jerusalem lies in ruins, and its gates have been burned with fire. Come, let us rebuild the wall of Jerusalem, and we will no longer be in disgrace'"* (Nehemiah 2:17). Nehemiah expressed to them his clear vision. Here was one man, with just a handful of people, who was planning to do a project that would take thousands of people to accomplish. Yet he said, "Let's do it. Let's rebuild this wall." He was starting out with a seeming impossibility, but he said, "Let's start."

You can't tell your plan to everyone right away.

Remember the principle of potential? It's not what you need that is important. Starting with what you have makes your vision successful because God will take care of the rest. I know you have some great ideas. Start right where you are and go where you need to go by making a plan and beginning to implement it.

Acknowledge God's Work in Your Life

Second, Nehemiah said, *"I also told them about the gracious hand of my God upon me and what the king had said to me"* (Nehemiah 2:18). I like the fact that Nehemiah told them that. He gave credit to God for the vision, and in the process also built up the faith of those who would work on the project. The vision needed to be passed along to them. They would need to exercise their own faith if they were to fulfill their personal visions within this larger vision that God had given to Nehemiah. The statement also shows that Nehemiah was so sure that his vision was from God and that the Lord was with him that he was able to say, in effect, "God told me to do this." Nehemiah wasn't guessing about what he should do. I hope you feel the same way about your dream.

Your Plan Is Material for Your Prayers

Moreover, when you put your plan on paper, you will find that you have plenty of material for your prayers. You can't fulfill your dream by yourself. You must have God's help. If your prayer time is short, maybe it's because you have nothing specific to pray about. If you develop a plan, however, you will never have enough time for prayer. There will always be something for which to call on your faith and to believe God.

Your Plan Will Enable You to Fulfill Your Destiny

In Deuteronomy 30:19, God told the people, *"I have set before you life and death, blessings and curses. Now choose life."* In other words, He was saying, "Stop procrastinating and hoping you will eventually get somewhere in life. Decide whether you're going to get a curse or a blessing. Decide whether you're going to die or live." Jesus said in Revelation 3:15–16,

> *I know your deeds, that you are neither cold nor hot. I wish you were either one or the other! So, because you are lukewarm—neither hot nor cold—I am about to spit you out of my mouth.*

You were designed for destiny. Make a plan and fulfill it.

Are you going to make a plan, or are you going to procrastinate on your dream and drift along, ending up wherever the lukewarm tide takes you? You were not designed to drift. You were designed for destiny. Make a plan and fulfill it.

Action Steps to Fulfilling Vision

- Do you know the answers to the questions "Who am I?" and "Where am I going?" Start the process of developing a blueprint for your vision by writing down answers to these questions.

- Start thinking about where you want to be one, five, ten, twenty, thirty years from now. Jot down your ideas and continue to think and pray about them.

- Read chapter seventeen, "How to Write Your Personal Vision Plan," and begin to write out the specifics of your plan.

Chapter Principles

1. To be successful, you must have a clear plan.

2. If you don't have a plan, God doesn't have anything specific to direct you in.

3. *"To man belong the plans of the heart, but from the LORD comes the reply of the tongue"* (Proverbs 16:1). God leaves the planning up to the heart of the person, but He will provide the explanation as to how the vision will be accomplished.

4. *"In his heart a man plans his course, but the LORD determines his steps"* (Proverbs 16:9).

5. When a person receives an idea from God, it must be cultivated soon or the idea often goes away.

6. Many opportunities come to people, but they have no plan in place that would enable them to make something out of them.

7. If you don't have a plan for your life, you have nothing to refer to when you want to make sure you are on track.

8. You must secure for yourself the answer to the question "Who am I?" You will never become really successful in your life if you don't have a clear idea of your own identity in God.

9. You must answer the question, "Where am I going?" Once you learn God's purpose, you can start planning effectively because you will be able to plan with focus.

10. A vision becomes a plan when it is captured, fleshed out, and written down.

11. You can't tell your plan to everyone because some people won't be able to handle it while you're making it.

12. Your dream is worth writing down. If God gave it to you, it deserves to be done.

13. Your plan is material for your prayers.

14. Your plan will enable you to fulfill your destiny.

Chapter Seven

Principle #4: Possess the Passion of Vision

FOR THE PEOPLE WORKED WITH ALL THEIR HEART.
—NEHEMIAH 4:6

The fourth principle for fulfilling personal vision is that you'll never be successful without passion. Passionate people are those who have discovered something more important than life itself. Jesus told His disciples, in essence, "If you are not willing to take up death and follow Me, then you can't be My disciples; you can't go on with Me." (See Luke 14:27.) He also said, in effect, "If you seek to save your life, you will lose it. Yet if you are willing to lose it for My vision of your life, you will truly live." (See Matthew 16:25.) Giving up false visions and ambition for your genuine vision is the path to true life.

How Badly Do You Want Your Vision?

Are you hungry for your vision? How badly do you want what you're going after? Passion is stamina that says, "I'm going to go after this, no matter what happens. If I have to wait ten years, I'm going to get it." Again, let me say especially to young people that if you want to go all the way to your dream, you can't sit back and expect everything to be easy. You must have purpose that produces passion. You must have the attitude of those who worked on the wall with Nehemiah: *"So we rebuilt the wall till all of it reached half its height, for the people worked with all their heart"* (Nehemiah 4:6).

Remember that, after Nehemiah saw in his heart a vision of the rebuilt wall, he returned to his job, but he was no longer satisfied with it. He was depressed until he was working on the vision. The depression came from his passion for change. I believe that Nehemiah was the kind of man who couldn't hide what he felt. He was sad because he didn't like the way the future looked for his people.

You must put your whole heart into your vision.

When you have a vision, you are sad about where you are because you want to be where your true joy is. People who are satisfied with a lesser existence, however, will never go where they need to be. Not only sadness at your present conditions, but also anger, can drive you to a new vision and take you to new horizons. You will never be successful until you are angry about not doing what you know you should be doing. If you're happy about what you're doing, you're going to end up settling right there.

Vision Is the Precedent for Passion

One of the reasons I keep stressing your need for a clear guiding purpose in life is that vision is the precedent for passion. **The majority of people in the earth really have no passion for life because there is no vision in their hearts.** In 2 Corinthians, we find a unique passage that shows the passion Paul had for his vision. Some people had challenged Paul's right to be an apostle. They said Paul was not really called by God and that he was not worthy of the respect he was getting. They themselves were false apostles, yet they attacked Paul's credibility and spiritual qualifications and drew people away from the truth. Paul responded by addressing the Corinthian believers who were being led away from faith in Jesus Christ by these false apostles. He wrote that, even if what he was about to say sounded ridiculous and foolish, he would say it anyway to prove he was an apostle so that they would return to the true Gospel:

> *Are* [these other men] *Hebrews? So am I. Are they Israelites? So am I. Are they Abraham's descendants? So am I. Are they servants of Christ? (I am out of my mind to talk like this.) I am more. I have worked much harder, been in prison more frequently, been flogged more severely, and been exposed to death again and again. Five times I received from the Jews the forty lashes minus one. Three times I was beaten with rods, once I was stoned, three times I was shipwrecked, I spent a night and a day in the open sea, I have been constantly on the move. I have been in danger from rivers, in danger from bandits, in danger from my own countrymen, in danger from Gentiles; in danger in the city, in danger in the country, in danger at sea; and in danger from false brothers. I have labored and toiled and have often gone without sleep; I have known hunger and thirst and have often gone without food; I have been cold and naked. Besides everything else, I face daily the pressure of my concern for all the churches.* (2 Corinthians 11:22–28)

Why did Paul give a list of problems and tribulations as part of the proof that he was a genuine apostle? He was saying, in effect, "If the vision and assignment I received wasn't real, do you think I'd go through all those hardships?"

Paul paid a price for the vision, but his passion enabled him to do it. You are passionate and you are real if you stay steady under pressure. You know your vision is from God when you are still at it once the storm clears. **It's easy to get excited about a vision, but it's harder to be faithful to it.** Faithfulness to vision is one of the marks of its legitimacy.

Paul had amazing academic credentials. He was envied by the best. This gifted young man had great power in the religious community and could have been a prominent Pharisee. He also could have had an easy life. His father was a merchant and a Roman citizen, and Paul was born with that citizenship. He was so set up to be successful that he could have made it in any category or profession. He really could have been a first-class success story. However, Paul said, "I'm going to jail, I'm going to be whipped, I'm going to go through a myriad of problems because the vision God showed me is more important than anything else in my life."

Faithfulness to vision is one of the marks of its legitimacy.

If someone who had the respect of everyone in the community and could have had any job he wanted was willing to go through all that, he had to have vision. Can you put that list of tribulations after your name and say you have gone through what Paul went through for the sake of your vision? Paul was driven and determined to serve Jesus Christ. He had previously sought to persecute the church, but now he was willing to go through persecution himself for the sake of Jesus. Why? He was clear about his vision.

In Acts 26, Paul was on trial before King Agrippa. As he told the king about the purpose that Jesus Christ had given him on the road to Damascus, he made a statement that is very important concerning people with vision:

> Then I asked, 'Who are you, Lord?' 'I am Jesus, whom you are persecuting,' the Lord replied. 'Now get up and stand on your feet. I have appeared to you to appoint you as a servant and as a witness of what you have seen of me and what I will show you. I will rescue you from your own people and from the Gentiles. I am sending you to them to open their eyes and turn them from darkness to light, and from the power of Satan to God, so that they may receive forgiveness of sins and a place among those who are sanctified by faith in me.' (Acts 26:15–18)

Paul summed up his account by saying, "So then, King Agrippa, I was not disobedient to the vision from heaven" (v. 19). He said that God had given him a clear guiding vision, which was to preach the Gospel to the Gentiles, and that he was not disobedient to it. He reiterated this vision to Timothy: *"For this purpose I was appointed a herald and an apostle—I am telling the truth, I am not lying—and a teacher of the true faith to the Gentiles"* (1 Timothy 2:7).

Passion means that what I believe is bigger than what I see.

Paul knew what his purpose in life was, and that is what kept him going through all his struggles. When your vision is from God, nothing can stop you. It doesn't matter if people talk about you. You can even be shipwrecked, beaten, and starved if you are bent on accomplishing your vision. Why did Paul keep getting up every time they stoned him? He knew he had to go to the Gentiles in obedience to the vision and command he had received from God. Vision is the source of passion.

Passion for Vision Overcomes Resistance

If you're going to be what you see in your mind, if you're going to go after what's in your heart, believe me, there will be resistance. The only way to overcome that resistance is to have passion for your vision. When you are truly passionate about your dream, you can stand strong when trouble comes. **Persistence will keep you moving forward, yet you need passion to feed your persistence.**

Passion is a desire that is stronger than death. You can't sleep, eat, or stop until you satisfy it. If you can stop what you're doing and still be happy, then you're not passionate about it. If you can be discouraged by someone telling you no or the bank refusing you money, then you don't have passion. Passion meets every problem. It says things such as these: "You may say 'no,' but I know it really means 'wait.'" "Even though you haven't come around to my idea now, you will later." "Even though you stop me now, I'm eventually going to jump this wall." "If you kill me, I'll rise and do it again."

113

A passionate person gets up in the morning and says, "Good morning, Lord! Here I am! Thank you for another day that will take me one step closer to where I want to go." Passion means that, no matter how tough things are, what I believe is bigger than what I see. It is an urge that is deeper than any resistance it might encounter. It is a goal to win that is bigger than the desire to quit.

Many people fail because they give up the first time they fall down.

People stop too soon. They don't win because they give up when they fall down the first time. Do you stop at the least resistance? Remember, passion says, "You might as well give up, because I'm not going to quit. If you knock me down, I'm going to get up. If you knock me down again, I'm going to get up again. I'm going to keep getting up until you get tired of knocking me down." Get up and get on with it! There is no life without passion. In Romans 1:14, Paul said, "'I am obligated' to do the work God told me to do." He just had to do it. It was God's will for his life, and he was *eager to preach the gospel* (v. 15). He couldn't wait to do it. A person of passion is always eager to fulfill his vision.

Passion Is Willing to Pay the Price

Sometimes, others will come and be a part of what you're doing and then say "This vision isn't real" because they don't know what the vision is costing you. Do you remember John Mark, the young man who joined Paul and Barnabas on a missionary journey? John Mark was a very excited and zealous young man. He worked with Paul and Barnabas until a certain point when he decided to leave them and return to Jerusalem. Later, when John Mark wanted to accompany them on another journey, Paul said no because he felt John Mark had deserted them and the work. He was saying, in effect, "John Mark, you're telling us you are with us in this vision, yet you can't handle the pressure, the tough times, the rigors of the work. I want people who will come with me through the fire and say, 'We did it together.'" (See Acts 12:25–13:13; 15:36–40.)

When you capture your vision and stay with it, you will be rewarded.

Barnabas ended up going with John Mark on a separate journey, and Paul asked Silas to join him. In Philippi, Paul and Silas were beaten and imprisoned when some men incited a mob against them. Silas could have told the magistrates that he didn't know Paul. Perhaps he could have escaped association as Peter did when he said about Jesus, *"I don't know the man!"* (Matthew 26:72, 74). Yet Silas was committed to the vision. If Paul went to jail, he would go to jail, too. I want you to know that the prison they were thrown into wasn't an ordinary lockup. Matthew Henry described this *"inner cell"* (Acts 16:24) as a "dungeon, into which none were usually put but condemned malefactors, dark at noon-day, damp and cold, dirty, it is likely, and every way offensive."* Yet this was the place where Paul and Silas sang hymns! (See Acts 16:16–25.) Passion is willing to pay the price.

Passion Keeps You Focused

One other crucial aspect of passion is that it helps you to stay focused on your vision. You can see this principle at work in churches. Wherever there is no vision, there is often fighting, gossiping, murmuring, backbiting, and complaining. When churches are full of complaints, that is evidence that the vision has left them. Vision preoccupies people to the point that they have no time to gossip or get angry at the pastor or complain about his preaching. The same phenomenon can be seen in marriages. One of the reasons why there are so many problems in marriages today is that couples have lost their joint vision. We

---

* *Matthew Henry's Commentary on the Whole Bible*, vol. 6 (Peabody, MA: Hendrickson Publishers, Inc., 1991), 170.

must rediscover the passion of working together for a common purpose and vision.

Defy the Odds

If you become passionate about your vision, you can defy the odds and persevere to the fulfillment of your goals. Whenever you are tempted to quit too soon or to stay down when life knocks you over, remember the examples of Nehemiah and Paul. Capture your vision and stay with it, and you will be rewarded with seeing that vision become a reality, no matter what might try to come against it.

Action Steps to Fulfilling Vision

- Ask yourself, "How hungry am I for my vision? How badly do I want what I'm going after?"

- What evidence of a passion for vision do you see in your life?

- Do you generally give up the first time you fall down? In what ways might you have become complacent about your vision? What will you do to regain your passion for your dreams?

Chapter Principles

1. You cannot be successful without passion.

2. Passionate people have discovered something more important than life itself.

3. Vision is the precedent for passion.

4. A vision will always be tested by tribulation.

5. Faithfulness to vision is one of the marks of its legitimacy.

6. Passion means that no matter how tough things are, what you believe is bigger than what you see.

7. A person of passion is always eager to fulfill his vision.

8. Passion keeps you focused on your vision.

Chapter Eight
Principle #5:
Develop the Faith of Vision

SIGHT IS A FUNCTION OF THE EYES, WHILE VISION IS A
FUNCTION OF THE HEART.

The fifth principle is that you must develop the faith of vision. Sight is a function of the eyes, while vision is a function of the heart.

The greatest gift that God gave humankind is not the gift of sight, but the gift of vision. You have probably heard of the great author and wonderful entrepreneur Helen Keller, who became blind, deaf, and mute as a result of an illness when she was only eighteen months old. She was a powerful, remarkable woman who impacted her whole generation, and she still influences us today. In her old age, she was interviewed by a news anchor about her life. Part of their conversation went something like this: Communicating his questions to her through Braille, he asked, "Miss Keller, is there anything worse than being blind?" She paused for a moment and, in her very unique way of talking, said, "What's worse than being blind is having sight without vision."

What a perceptive woman! This woman, who could not see physically, had more vision and accomplishments than the majority of those in her generation who had sight. Her books are still read today, and her poetry is wonderful. Helen Keller didn't spend her years being angry and blaming God for her blindness and deafness. No, she was able to live a full life because she had vision in her heart. As the saying goes, "Eyes that look are common, but eyes that see are rare."

Vision Sees Things as They Could Be

I am convinced that most people have sight but no vision. Physical sight is the ability to see things as they are. Vision is the capacity to see things as they could be, and that takes faith.

The Bible says, *"As* [a person] *thinks in his heart, so is he"* (Proverbs 23:7 NKJV). We must never let what our eyes see determine what our hearts believe. *"For we walk* ["*live*" NIV] *by faith, not by sight"* (2 Corinthians 5:7 NKJV). In other words, we are to walk according to what is in our hearts. We are to let what is in our hearts dictate how we see life.

Never let what your eyes see determine what your heart believes.

God told Abraham something that could be seen, believed, and achieved only through the eyes of vision: He told him that inside him was a nation. He and Sarah were already elderly, and Sarah had been barren throughout their marriage. However, God said, in effect, "I see a nation in you. Everyone else is looking at your barrenness, but I see a nation of descendants as numerous as the stars in the sky and the sand on the shore." (See Genesis 11:29–30; 12:1–3; 17:1–19.)

When we have vision, we are governed by the faith God has put in our hearts. Hebrews 11:1 says that *"faith is the substance of things hoped for, the evidence of things not seen* [that you cannot see]" (NKJV). Therefore, **I would define faith as vision in the heart.** Faith is seeing the future in the present. When you have faith, you can see things you hope to have and achieve.

Seeing by Faith

If you are operating by sight, you see the problems and challenges all around you. You see how many bills you have to pay; you see that your company is downsizing; you see things that threaten your security. Sight without vision is dangerous because it has no hope. Many people have been living by sight alone, and that's one reason they have all kinds of medical problems—muscle tension, migraines, high blood pressure, heart disease, ulcers, tumors, and so on. Living by sight can kill you. Life is so full of depressing things that you need to learn to live by vision and see with the eyes of faith.

Remember that sight is the ability to see things as they are, and vision is the ability to see things as they could be. I like to go a step further and define vision this way: Vision is the ability to see things as they *should* be.

Sight without vision is dangerous because it has no hope.

Maybe you are going through a hard time right now and you're disheartened. You've lost your vision edge. Perhaps this is because of your surroundings. Sometimes, the environments we live in are not the best for fostering vision. What people say to us is not always encouraging and can be very *dis*couraging. I have been tempted to be disillusioned and discouraged many times. Even though we know that the discouraging things we see and hear are temporary, they still can distress and depress us. We must keep our visions constantly before us, however, because **the visions in our hearts are greater than our environments.** God gave us vision so we would not have to live by what we see.

Our spirits were designed to operate as God operates. In Genesis 1:26, God said, *"Let us make man in our image, in our likeness."* The word *"image"* refers to moral and spiritual character, while the phrase *"in our likeness"* means "to function like." In other words, we were created to live according to the nature of God and to function as He functions in the world.

The Bible is very clear that *"without faith it is impossible to please God"* (Hebrews 11:6). If you try to function in any other

121

way than faith, you will malfunction. That is why worry is ungodly and fear makes your vision short-circuit. You were never meant to be afraid.

Thoughts are the most *important*, and words are the most *powerful*.

Jesus was filled with faith, and He was the calmest person on earth. He slept soundly in the middle of a storm. When His frightened disciples woke Him up, He asked them, *"Do you still have no faith?"* (Mark 4:40). He was telling them, "If you have faith, you'll be able to sleep during a storm, as well." You may be saying, "This doesn't sound very practical." It is, however. I have been living this way—by faith instead of fear—for over twenty years, and it's been so much fun. I don't worry for very long about anything because I believe that, ultimately, everything is on my side. Even the schemes of the devil work to my benefit. All things work for my good because I am called according to God's purpose. (See Romans 8:28.)

The Creative Power of Faith

How does faith work? To understand the answer to this question, we need to examine more closely how God functions. In Jeremiah 1:12, God declared, *"I am watching to see that my word is fulfilled."* The *New American Standard Bible* says it this way: *"I am watching over My word to perform it."* As this verse—along with many others throughout the Bible—demonstrates, God always brings His words into being. What did God use to create the universe? He used words. All through the account of Creation, we read, *"God said"* (Genesis 1:3, 6, 9, 11, 14, 20, 24, 26). God had an idea for the universe, and then He saw or visualized it. Finally, He *spoke* His idea into existence. The result was that everything God saw in His mind's eye for the earth and the rest of the universe became visible reality in the physical world. God created everything by speaking His thoughts into being.

Nothing on earth is more important than a thought. Thoughts are more important than words because words are produced from thoughts. Yet while thoughts are the most *important* things on earth, words are the most *powerful*. This point is crucial to understand because, while thoughts design a future, words create that future. Nothing happens until you start talking about it. You can think about something for twenty years, but that will not bring it to pass. Creative power is not in thoughts alone. It is in the words (and actions) that come from them. Whether those words are spoken or written, they are full of creative power.

You can undermine your vision through negative thoughts and words.

Therefore, when you speak words expressing what you see in your vision, your words become creative power to help bring that vision to fruition. However, there is a negative aspect to this truth, as well: You can undermine your vision by what you continually say about yourself, such as "I'm fat," "I'm slow," "I'm not intelligent," "I'm a timid person," "I don't like people," "I'm a failure," or "I'll always have a mortgage." I am. I am. I am. You will become everything you constantly declare about yourself. That is the power of words.

Compounding this problem is the fact that the devil knows God and His ways very well. Satan knows that the key to creating anything is having a clear vision of it and speaking it into existence. He wants you to speak negative rather than positive things so that your effectiveness for God's kingdom will be negated. We can help protect our visions by guarding what we say.

If you want to fulfill your vision, you must speak differently than you have been. Instead of saying, "I'll always have a mortgage," say, "I'm going to be debt free." Can you say that? You may have been imagining that you don't owe any bills, but you have to start saying it, as well. Say, *"My God will meet all* [my] *needs according to his glorious riches in Christ Jesus"* (Philippians 4:19), then pray, "Lord, please perform Your Word." You have to speak. A vision doesn't have any power until you talk about it.

Faith Sees Problems as Opportunities

Life is the way you see it. When you begin to see with the eyes of faith, you will understand how to make your vision a reality. There is a story of a man and his friend who visited India years ago. They were walking down the streets of Bombay and saw the thousands of poor people on the streets. Hundreds lay on cardboard boxes in the gutters or under the bridges. Filthy people were begging along the streets. There were poor people by the thousands walking barefoot.

The man said to his friend, "Look at these people. Isn't it a sad sight? They're without shoes. Thousands of barefoot people. What a pity. Isn't it a shame that we have so much at home in our country while these people are poor and without shoes. I'll never forget this sight. I have to tell my wife about this." He continued to talk about how poor they were and about their bare feet. By this time, his friend had already taken out a piece of paper and was writing down some notes. He had started working out a plan of how to ship shoes over to India and how to manufacture shoes in India. Instead of saying, "Look at the bare feet," he was saying, "Look at the feet that need shoes!" Today his enterprise is one of the largest shoe companies in America. One man saw bare feet. Another man saw an opportunity for a much-needed business. It's all in how you see.

Let me give you another illustration of this truth. Some years ago, a pastor said to me, "Dr. Munroe, I am from Vermont, and there isn't anything up there. There is nothing but maple trees, cows, and snow. There isn't anything happening in the town where I'm from, and I want to do something for God. I'm going to move down south, build a nice church, and do a work for God." I listened to him for a while and then said, "Think about it. If there isn't any other church to go to in your town, you have a great opportunity to build the most dynamic church in Vermont." He looked at me and said, "Yeah!" Today, he has the largest church in his town. We must not only have sight but also vision.

You can see every problem as an opportunity for ministry, service, or business. That is really how Bahamas Faith Ministries International got started. The number one problem of people in developing nations is ignorance. God raised up BFMI to be one of the solutions to that problem: to bring knowledge, training, and information to the Third World. The organization was birthed to help solve a problem that affects 3.8 billion people. I believe with all my heart that the Bahamas will become known as a center for education and training, not just sun and sand. There are going to be all kinds of universities, training schools, and opportunities to grow intellectually. That's the vision God has placed in my heart.

Great Thinking Precedes Great Achievement

Successful men and women who have impressed and impacted their generations weren't "lucky." They didn't just stumble on greatness. They thought great things and expected great things, and greatness found them. Big thinking precedes great achievement. You don't need to *be* big to think great thoughts. You need to think great thoughts to become big. That is the faith of vision.

You don't need to *be* big to think great thoughts. You need to think great thoughts to become big.

You must realize that ideas control the world. Ideas are so powerful that many nations are ruled by the thoughts of men who have long since died. When I went to college, most of the books I read were by people who are no longer living. I spent thousands of dollars studying their ideas. A vision is an idea that is so powerful it can live beyond the grave. Your own vision should outlive you. In order for that to happen, however, you can't keep your ideas to yourself. You must clearly conceive and express them.

I'll never forget the time I was grappling with the possibility of writing books. I told God that I didn't want to write because so many others were writing books, and I didn't want to do it just because everybody else was doing it. I wanted my teaching to be real and genuine. For months, I struggled with this issue because publishers had been calling me telling me that they had listened to audio tapes of my teachings and had seen my television program. They said, "You have many ideas that need to be shared with millions of people. Why don't you write a book?" At first, I told them, "I don't want to write a book. I'm happy just teaching." However, when I was preparing my notes one night for a teaching, I felt as if the Lord was saying to me, "If you do not write, what you know will die with you. If you write down the ideas that I have given you, however, your words will live on after you are gone."

Do You Have Sight or Vision?

Your success or failure is determined by how you see. Jesus continually dealt with the sight of the disciples because their sight got them into trouble so often. He wanted them to move from sight to vision, and that is why He taught them about faith through life illustrations such as the fig tree, the feeding of the five thousand, and the raising of Lazarus. (See, for example, Matthew 21:19–22; Mark 6:34–44; John 11:1–44.)

The faith of vision is crucial because the way you see things determines how you think and act and, therefore, whether or not your vision will become reality. Proverbs 23:7 says, *"As* [a person] *thinks in his heart, so is he"* (NKJV). Do you have sight or vision?

Action Steps to Fulfilling Vision

- What is your answer to the question that concluded this chapter: Do you have sight or vision?

- Are you thinking and speaking in positive or negative terms in relation to your vision?

- Choose one aspect of your vision and practice speaking words of faith regarding it.

Chapter Principles

1. Sight is a function of the eyes, while vision is a function of the heart.

2. Sight is the ability to see things as they are, while vision is the ability to see things as they could (or *should*) be.

3. We must never let what our eyes see determine what our hearts believe.

4. Faith is vision in the heart.

5. Sight without vision is dangerous because it has no hope.

6. The visions in our hearts are greater than our environments.

7. God gave us vision so we would not have to live by what we see.

8. We were created to live according to the way God functions. God functions through faith and His Word.

9. While thoughts are the most *important* things on earth, words are the most *powerful*. Thoughts design a future, but words create that future.

10. Whether words are spoken or written, they are full of creative power.

11. Faith sees problems as opportunities.

12. Great thinking precedes great achievement.

13. You don't need to *be* big to think great thoughts. You need to think great thoughts to become big. That is the faith of vision.

14. Ideas control the world.

15. A vision is an idea that is so powerful it can live beyond the grave.

16. In order for your vision to outlive you, you can't keep your ideas to yourself. You must clearly conceive and express them.

17. The faith of vision is crucial because the way you see things determines how you think and act and, therefore, whether or not your vision will become reality.

Chapter Nine

Principle #6: Understand the Process of Vision

IN HIS HEART A MAN PLANS HIS COURSE,
BUT THE LORD DETERMINES HIS STEPS.
—PROVERBS 16:9

The sixth principle is that we must understand the process of vision. God has a plan for each of our lives, yet He brings those plans to pass in a gradual way. I'm learning that God tells us where we are going with our visions, but He rarely tells us exactly how He will take us there. He gives us purpose but doesn't explain the full process.

Proverbs 16:9 says, *"In his heart a man plans his course, but the LORD determines his steps."* Notice the word *"steps."* God didn't say He would direct our leaps, but rather our steps. There is no hurried way to get to God's vision. He leads us step-by-step, day-by-day, through tribulations, trials, and character-building opportunities as He moves us toward our dreams. Why does God lead us in this way? Because He doesn't want us only to win; He wants us to win with style. God's desire is to fashion people with character and battle scars who can say, "God didn't just hand me this vision. I have qualified for it."

The Route Prepares Us for the Destination

Sometimes, we become impatient with God's process because we can see our destinations, and we want to arrive there tomorrow. However, God says, "No, I have a route that will get you there." Even though this route may seem long, it is not designed to keep us from our destinations; it is designed to prepare us for them.

At the time when we receive our visions, we are not yet ready for them. We don't yet have the ability to handle the big things that we're dreaming. We don't have the experience or the character for them. God could accomplish quickly what He desires to do through us, yet He wants to prepare us to receive and work in our visions.

At the time when we receive our visions, we are not yet ready for them.

You must learn to train for what God has already told you is coming. You don't need to worry about whether or not it is going to come. If He has promised that it is coming, then it is. Yet you must stay on course if you're going to follow the work God has called you to do. Stay in the seat where God has placed you, put on your seat belt, and hang on until He brings the vision to pass. It will be realized, but you must wait on Him.

We ask God, "Why do I need to go this way? I don't like this route." He answers that the route is going to do two things for us:

1. develop our character
2. produce responsibility in us

We weren't born with those things, so we have to learn them. Moreover, if God were to show us the route to where we are going, we might say, "That's okay, God. You can keep the vision. I'll stay right where I am."

Let's look at the life of Joseph as an example. When he was only seventeen years old, he had a dream from God in which his father, mother, and brothers were kneeling down before him. (See Genesis 37:9–10.) Joseph thought to himself, "Yes! I like this dream." He saw himself up on a throne with a whole kingdom at his feet. In his mind, he was King Joseph.

God had given him a vision, yet He didn't tell him how he was going to get there. Suppose God had said, "Joseph, you're going to become a great ruler, and here is what I have planned to get you there. First, your brothers are going to tear your favorite clothes right off your back. Second, they are going to throw you into a pit. Third, they are going to sell you as a slave. Fourth, your master's wife is going to lie about you, accusing you of rape. Fifth, your master is going to have you put in jail, where you will be forgotten for a long time. However, eventually, you'll get there." If God had said that, Joseph probably would have replied, "I'll tell you what. I'll just stay a shepherd. I'm very happy where I am right now."

God's ways of getting us where we need to go are often different from what we expect.

Some of you are in the midst of the vision process and are wondering, "Where's the vision God promised me? Where are all those big dreams He showed me five years ago? The business I was working for closed down. I lost my job, and then I lost my house. This doesn't look anything like the vision He showed me." You are beginning to wonder if there is a God in heaven. Joseph likely felt the same way during his ordeals. He found himself sitting in a pit when, just a few days earlier, he had seen himself on a throne. He was probably thinking, "Where is the God who showed me that dream?" I believe God's reply to Joseph was something like this: "I'm with you in the pit, and I'm working on your character because you can't rule well without it."

131

Suppose Joseph hadn't learned self-control through all his hardships? When Potiphar's wife tried to seduce him, he might have given in to the temptation. Instead, because he had had to learn discipline and reliance on God, he could be trusted in such a situation. God's ways of getting us where we need to go are often different from what we expect, but there is always a good reason for them.

Do you really believe that God sees and knows everything? If you do, then you have to trust that your hardships are part of His perfect plan for you. If you lost your job this morning, your first question may be, "How am I going to pay the mortgage?" Yet God will say to you, "Do you believe I know you?" If you answer, "Yes, Lord," He will say, "Good. It's part of the plan. I'm working on your character. Let me take care of your mortgage."

Life's hardships are part of God's perfect plan for us and our visions.

Let's look at another example. What if God had said to Moses, while he was still one of the most powerful men in Egypt as the adopted son of Pharaoh's daughter, "I have raised you up to be a deliverer to bring My people out of Egypt into the Promised Land, but this is how it will transpire: In your zeal to protect My people, you will rashly murder an Egyptian, and you will have to flee into the wilderness and become a mere shepherd. Then, when you become the leader of the Israelites, they are going to infuriate you. They are going to murmur and complain. They are going to revolt against you. As a matter of fact, because of your reaction to them, you will disobey Me, and you won't even make it into the Promised Land." I think Moses would have said, "Lord, You can keep both the people and Pharaoh. I think I'll pass on this vision."

We think that, just because we're going through difficult times, God has stopped working to fulfill our purposes. Yet they are still coming. **God is working on us, preparing us for our purposes through the process.** However, we often sit back and say, "Why is it taking so long? Why do I have to go through all this?" That attitude of complaint and lack of faith is exactly what God is trying to work out of you. He doesn't want you to go into your promised land dragging bad attitudes behind you. He is working for your good.

What about Daniel? God appointed him to be a prophet and allowed him to see visions of future events, including the end times, yet God didn't tell him that he would be thrown into a lion's den for obeying Him! Again, God's plan to get you where you are meant to be is unpredictable. He doesn't tell you about it because you might be tempted to quit.

What about Paul? God told him, essentially, "You will be an apostle to the Gentiles for Me. You will preach to kings." (See Acts 9:15.) Paul might have thought, "That sounds pretty good." However, if God had told him about the fastings, the whippings, the stonings, the hunger, and the prisons, Paul might have said, "I think I'll stay in Jerusalem rather than going on that road to Damascus." As it was, after his conversion, God did warn Paul through Ananias, *I will show him how much he must suffer for my name*" (v. 16).

What about Jesus? When the Son of God was born, wise men came to visit Him. They bowed down before Him, calling Him a king. Yet what a process He had to go through to get to that throne! In the Garden of Gethsemane, Jesus began to feel the burden, and He prayed, in effect, "Isn't there any other way?" (See Matthew 26:36–44.) He felt what you are feeling. You might say, "Isn't there another way to start a business?" God will answer, "No. This is the way I am taking you. You want to have a shoe store? Good. I want you to start by working in one." Or you might ask, "Isn't there a better way of opening my own restaurant?" and God will say, "You'll have your restaurant, but first you have to learn to cook for someone else. This is your route. I'm working on your character and your training." Sometimes, we want the vision without being qualified for it.

You may not face a life-or-death situation, as some of God's people have, but you will have challenges and difficulties in one degree or another as you move toward the fulfillment of your vision. That is why I want you to be aware of the process of vision and be prepared for it. I don't want you to give up on your vision prematurely. **God will continually fulfill a little more of your dream until it comes to pass.** It will culminate in His timing. This is the will of God for you. Lamentations 3:26 says, *"It is good to wait quietly for the salvation of the LORD."*

Live by faith as you move through the process of vision.

I wrote earlier that Monday mornings are depressing for many people because they hate their jobs. Yet such jobs can serve a purpose in God's plan. God places us in jobs that will prepare us for our life's work. Remember that a job is a preoccupation on the way to true occupation.

If you are frustrated with your job, you need to stay there unless God directs otherwise, realizing that it is not your permanent position. I'm very glad for each of the jobs I have had, because they all prepared me for what I'm doing right now. What I am doing now is so fulfilling that I could do it for the rest of my life. Therefore, submit yourself to your job, learn what you're supposed to learn, and get all the knowledge that you can from it, because you're going to move on in a little while.

Purpose gives your job meaning. Being in a pit and in prison didn't stop Joseph because he saw himself as a ruler, and he knew that one day his vision would be fulfilled. God's purpose in your heart is what enables you to keep moving forward.

The Vision Will Not Prove False

The prophet Habakkuk asked God, *"How long, O LORD, must I call for help, but you do not listen?"* (Habakkuk 1:2). He was referring to all the problems and difficulties that were taking place in his nation. There was disorder, corruption, and murder. The Lord's answer to him was this:

> *Write down the revelation and make it plain on tablets so that a herald may run with it. For the revelation awaits an appointed time; it speaks of the end and will not prove false. Though it linger, wait for it; it will certainly come and will not delay.... But the righteous will live by his faith.* (Habakkuk 2:2–4)

The vision that you have received awaits an appointed time. It speaks concerning the end—not the end of life or the end of the age, but the end, or fulfillment, of your dream. *"It speaks of the end and will not prove false."* In other words, God is saying, "If I gave you a vision, don't worry that it seems as if it isn't happening. It *will* come to pass." In the meantime, we are told that *"the righteous will live by his faith."*

This is where walking by faith and not by sight comes in. You must believe in what God has told you because it won't happen overnight. It will occur through a process of character development, which will come as you live by faith and inner vision—not by what you see.

Action Steps to Fulfilling Vision

- How has God used experiences in your life to build character in you?
- What character qualities has God shown you that you need to work on?
- List ways in which your job is preparing you for your life's work, such as skills, knowledge, and experience.

Chapter Principles

1. God has a plan for each of our lives, yet He brings those plans to pass in a gradual way.

2. God will tell you where you are going with your vision, but He will rarely tell you exactly how He will take you there.

3. There is no hurried way to get to God's vision.

4. At the time that we receive our visions, we are not yet ready for them.

5. The process of vision (1) develops our character and (2) produces responsibility in us.

6. God places us in jobs that will prepare us for our life's work.

7. The vision God has given you will come to pass. Until then, you are to live by faith.

Chapter Ten
Principle #7:
Set the Priorities of Vision

YOUR LIFE IS THE SUM TOTAL OF THE DECISIONS YOU
MAKE EVERY DAY.

Principle number seven is that, if you want to be successful, you must set priorities for yourself in relation to
your vision.

Our Decisions Are Based on Our Priorities

Understanding priority will help you accomplish your
dream because **priority is the key to effective decision-
making.** Both successful and unsuccessful people alike make
decisions every day that influence their chances of achieving
their visions. Whether they realize it or not, it is the nature
and quality of the choices they make that determine their success or failure.

Life is filled with alternatives; we are constantly bom-
barded with choices, and our preferences reveal who we are
and what we value in life. In fact, your life is the sum total of
the decisions you make every day. You have become what you
have decided for the last fifteen, twenty, or thirty years of your
life. What is perhaps even more significant, you can tell the
kind of life you're going to have in the future by the decisions

you are making today. In this sense, the future really is now. Sometimes, we believe that we can make bad choices today and make up for them later on. That thinking is in error. Whatever we are doing now is our tomorrow.

This is why *yes* and *no* are the most powerful words you will ever say. God wants you to be able to say them with precision because they will determine your destiny. You will be blessed by saying yes to what is in accordance with your vision and no to anything else.

Vision Focuses Your Priorities

In other words, if you want to fulfill your dream, you must fix your eyes on it and not get caught up in anything that won't take you there. You have to know how to maneuver between the alternatives of life, meaning that you have to learn how to prioritize. **When people don't succeed in their visions, it is often because they don't understand that prioritizing creates useful limits on their choices.**

Yes and *no* are the most powerful words you will ever say.

In 1 Corinthians 6:12, Paul wrote, *"'Everything is permissible for me'—but not everything is beneficial."* Even though we have permission to do everything and anything we want to, *"not everything is beneficial"* for us. The King James Version uses the word *"expedient,"* which means "appropriate," "suitable," or "desirable." Not everything is advantageous to you. You have to determine what is beneficial, and you have to define what is beneficial based on the needs of your vision.

The second part of 1 Corinthians 6:12 is a very powerful statement: *"'Everything is permissible for me'—but I will not be mastered by anything"* (emphasis added). The King James Version reads, *"I will not be brought under the power of any."* The Greek word translated *"power"* means "to control." Even though you can do anything in life, the only things that should master you are the things that will take you to your goal.

Just because something is a good thing does not necessarily mean it is beneficial to you. For example, when you are traveling along a highway, there are dozens of exits you might take. Is there such a thing as a "bad" exit? No, they're all good, legitimate routes. Many of them lead to helpful services, such as hotels, restaurants, or gas stations. Therefore, is there anything that makes an exit "bad" for you? Yes—if it doesn't lead to your desired destination. The same is true for the activities and people in your life. Something is beneficial if it relates to what you want to accomplish and takes you to your goal. Ask yourself, "What benefits me? What will move me toward my goal?"

Prioritize your life in keeping with your vision.

Obviously, the first thing that you would consider to be beneficial is your relationship with God. If you want to know where you're supposed to go in life, you have to establish a connection with the Person who gave you the assignment, who created you. It's no wonder the Bible says the greatest commandment is to love God first with all your heart, mind, soul (will), and strength. (See Mark 12:30.) When you do that, He reveals to you the assignment that you were born to fulfill. Once you are certain of where you are meant to go in life and have truly committed to it, then a lot of the extraneous things will fall away on their own.

After you capture your vision, you need to prioritize your life in keeping with that vision. You have to decide how many of the things that you are currently involved in are beneficial to your dream. There might not necessarily be anything wrong with them. They just may not be right for you to be involved in based on what you need to accomplish. There may be some good people in your life who are "bad" for you because they're distracting you from going where you want to go. There may be

139

some good books in your house that are wrong for you because they take your focus off your goal. You must come to the point where you focus on what is necessary to fulfill your dream. If you don't do that, you won't make it to the end of your vision.

Good versus Best

The key is that *the vision itself* decides what is good for you. You don't just do good things. You do things that are good for your vision.

Most of us know the difference between right and wrong. Therefore, your greatest challenge is not in choosing between good or bad but between *good* and *best*. A vision protects you from being misguided by good alternatives. It allows you to say no to lesser opportunities, even if there are certain benefits to them.

We can see a clear illustration of the principle of priorities in Jesus' reactions to the choices of Martha and Mary of Bethany:

> *As Jesus and his disciples were on their way, he came to a village where a woman named Martha opened her home to him. She had a sister called Mary, who sat at the Lord's feet listening to what He said. But Martha was distracted by all the preparations that had to be made. She came to him and asked, "Lord, don't you care that my sister has left me to do the work by myself? Tell her to help me!"* (Luke 10:38–40)

Martha had made a very good, honorable request: "What I'm doing is important, and I need help." What could be more important than preparing a meal for Jesus? Yet listen to the answer of the Lord: *"Martha, Martha....You are worried and upset about many things"* (v. 41). Jesus didn't say "bad" things, just *"many things."* He continued, *"But only one thing is needed. Mary has chosen what is better, and it will not be taken away from her"* (v. 42).

Jesus was saying, in effect, "You're doing what is good, Martha, but Mary has shifted into an area of life that I wish everyone would go to. Don't just do good things. Concentrate on what is best." Martha was so busy doing good things that she didn't do the right thing. When Jesus said, *"Mary has chosen what is better,"* what did He declare was *"better"*? It was *"only one thing"*—devotion to Jesus and His Word. This principle applies to both our relationship to God and our fulfillment of what He has given us to do. When you concentrate on one or two things, you have chosen the better way to live. You must find your calling and stay in it.

Your greatest challenge is not in choosing between good or bad but between *good* and *best*.

Many people have their own ideas about what they want to do for God, and this is why they keep drifting off in the wrong direction. It is easy to become preoccupied in doing things for God rather than doing what God has specifically told us to do. In the story of Martha and Mary, nowhere does it say that Jesus was hungry. It says just that Martha went about preparing food for Jesus. God doesn't want us to start anything, including doing good works for Him, until we consult Him. This is because He doesn't want us to work *for* Him, but *with* Him in partnership. We are *"God's fellow workers"* (2 Corinthians 6:1) or *"workers together with Him"* (NKJV).

Keep Your Eyes on the Mark

Jesus made it clear that Martha missed out on *"what is better"* because she was dwelling on the wrong things. **When someone sets his eyes on a goal and never takes them off it, he is guaranteed to reach that goal.**

When I was in Israel, the group I was traveling with spent an afternoon visiting a kibbutz. A kibbutz is a self-sufficient community. Everything the people need to live is found right there on the farm. As I walked the grounds and saw the beautiful fields where they grow their own food, I noticed that their tractors and combines were very modern. Then I saw a little field in a valley not too far from the kibbutz. A man was working in the field with just an ox hooked up to a plow.

I was intrigued with the sight, and I asked one of the men at the kibbutz, "What's he doing?" He answered, "Well, he's preparing the field to plant seed. As a matter of fact, he's planting seeds now. As the ox makes the furrow, he drops the seeds into the earth." I said, "He's using an animal, and he's using an old, outdated plow, but his field is just as perfect as yours, and you use modern machinery!" The man told me, "That guy's system is better than mine! Here's how he keeps his furrows completely straight. First, at the end of the field, he sets up little sticks and ties red or white flags on them. Then he goes back to the opposite end of the field, where he starts to plow. He sets his eyes on the little piece of cloth at the far end of the field as he controls the movements of the ox. If he didn't use the sticks, his furrows would be crooked."

When you take your eyes off the mark, you end up where you don't want to be.

Then he said something that put the whole thing into perspective for me: "That little stick is called 'the mark.'" That term took me back two thousand years to that same country, to that same area of Palestine, where Jesus had lived, and I understood what Jesus meant in Luke 9:62: *"No one who puts his hand to the plow and looks back is fit for service in the kingdom of God."* When you set your hand to the plow, you must put your eyes on the mark and not look to the left or to the right because you will inevitably move toward whatever you are looking at.

Do you remember when you were learning to ride a bicycle? You were told to look straight ahead because, wherever you looked, that's where you were going. If you looked down, you would fall down. Many of us have set markers in our lives—our visions—claiming that that is where we are headed, but then we keep looking everywhere except at our visions. It doesn't take too long before we're off course. Ten years later, we suddenly realize, "I really wanted to go back to school. What happened?" If we'd been in school in the first place, we could have graduated in just four years. We keep taking our eyes off the mark, and that is why we end up in places where we don't really want to be. We drift off course because we allow ourselves to be pulled in many different directions by all kinds of distractions. Again, we are busy with a number of activities rather than a single focused right thing to do.

In Matthew 11:30, Jesus said, *"My yoke is easy and my burden is light."* A yoke is a single piece of wood that joins two oxen together. It keeps them at the same pace and in the same position. Jesus also said, *"Come to me, all you who are weary and burdened, and I will give you rest. Take my yoke upon you and learn from me"* (vv. 28–29). We are to join with God's plan for our lives and let His yoke guide us. This means that, if He turns, we turn; if He stops, we stop. We stay with Him at the same pace and in the same position. This is the way we hit the mark.

Do What You Were Born to Do

Vision protects you from trying to do everything. The apostle Paul had a deep love and concern for the Jews. He wrote in Romans 9:3–4, *"For I could wish that I myself were cursed and cut off from Christ for the sake of my brothers, those of my own race, the people of Israel."* However, Paul knew that God hadn't called him to be an apostle to the Jews. They were his people, he was born from among them, and he was one of them, yet his purpose was to preach to the Gentiles: *"For this purpose I was appointed a herald and an apostle—I am telling the truth, I am not lying—and a teacher of the true faith to the Gentiles"* (1 Timothy 2:7). He knew what he was appointed for, and he stayed in his vision. Paul's vision was his motivating force: *"I am so eager to preach the gospel also to you who are at Rome"* (Romans 1:15).

Perhaps we become involved in too many things because we're trying to impress God and other people by showing them how much we are capable of doing. Yet we must remember that our gifts are the key to fulfilling our visions. If we spend time on things that we're not as gifted in, we will wear ourselves down to the point that, when we come back to our gifts, we are too tired to use them effectively.

Jesus Himself was born to do one main thing. He knew why He was manifested, and He kept His eyes completely fixed on His vision. He came to testify to the truth of God's kingdom and His plan of redemption for humankind and to die on the cross to accomplish that redemption.

How disciplined is your life in relation to your dream?

At one point, one of Jesus' closest friends tried to talk Him out of His vision. Peter said, in essence, "Master, You're talking about how You're going to die and how they're going to destroy You. Listen, I'm Your friend, so let me tell You something: *This shall never happen to you!*' (Matthew 16:22)." In other words, Peter was saying, "I don't want my Friend to die. If any man attempts to attack Him, he will first have to go through me!" Those sound like the words of a true friend, don't they? Peter wasn't saying anything bad, but it wasn't right based on Jesus' vision. Even your friends can be dangerous when they distract you from your dream. We have to realize that our enemy will try to use those nearest to us to divert us from the right path. Jesus rebuked the real threat that was behind Peter's statement when He said, *"Get behind me, Satan!"* (v. 23). Likewise, we must recognize the enemy's tactics when he works through those closest to us.

Vision Disciplines Your Choices

Vision is the key to an effective life because when you see your destination, it helps you to discipline your life in ways that train, prepare, and provide for your vision.

Proverbs 29:18 is often quoted but not fully understood: *"Where there is no vision, the people perish"* (KJV). The word in the

Hebrew for *"perish"* means "to throw off constraints." If you don't have vision, then there are no real restraints in your life. Yet, when you have vision, you are able to say no with dignity. The *New International Version* reads, *"Where there is no revelation, the people cast off restraint."* The use of the words *"revelation"* and *"restraint"* is very significant because the verse may be interpreted as meaning, "Where there is no vision, the people throw off self-control." **You will never be disciplined in your life until you have real vision.**

How disciplined is your own life in relation to your dream? Ask yourself questions such as these:

- *What am I using my energies on?* What are you putting your heart and soul into? Is it worth it, based on your purpose?

- *Where am I investing my money?* Your vision dictates where you put your resources. Are you buying things that are more expensive than you can afford and that you don't need? Are you so much in debt that you can't channel your money toward fulfilling the vision in your heart?

- *What movies and television programs am I watching?* If you know where you are going, you will choose to watch things that are related to your vision because you want to invest that time in your future.

- *What books am I reading?* Is what you're reading helping or hindering you? For example, if all you're reading is romance novels, you are living in a fantasy and not your true dream. You could be reading something that helps you in the knowledge or skills you need to fulfill your vision.

- *What hobbies am I pursuing?* You can choose to play games that prepare you for what you were born to do.

- *What am I taking into my body?* There are talented, gifted people who are dying prematurely because they consistently eat food that isn't good for them. If you're going to make it to the end of your vision,

145

you must take care of your health. Your vision may take twenty years to be fulfilled, so you need to start eating right and taking vitamins now. If you neglect your health, you will be more susceptible to sickness, and by the time you are halfway to your vision, you may be too ill to complete it (or no longer here).

- *What am I risking?* Are you abusing alcohol, drugs, or sex? If so, they could easily short-circuit your vision. For example, if you are a young woman who is being pressured into having premarital sex, think about how that might affect the fulfillment of your life's dream. Will it be easier to fulfill your goal if you have a baby out of wedlock or are infected with a sexually transmitted disease? If a young man starts to touch you inappropriately, tell him, "You are interfering with my future. Take me home right now." You must protect your vision.

- *What is my attitude toward life?* If you know where you're going, you can keep your attitude positive. When things go wrong, you can say, "That's okay. This is only temporary. I know where my true destination is." Paul said we should discipline our thoughts to think about what will build us up: *"Whatever is true, whatever is noble, whatever is right, whatever is pure, whatever is lovely, whatever is admirable—if anything is excellent or praiseworthy—think about such things"* (Philippians 4:8).

Choose to live well. Associate with people and be involved in things that are conducive to your dream.

"I Am Carrying on a Great Project"

Nehemiah made a statement that I believe everyone with vision should learn to make. It's one of the greatest statements of priority that I have ever read, either in the Bible, history, or anywhere else. Nehemiah was at a place where he had started to rebuild the wall. He had motivated the people by giving them a renewed purpose, he was able to communicate to them the necessity of doing this great project, and they were working hard at it. Yet, in Nehemiah 6:1, he was confronted by three men who wanted to prevent his vision from being fulfilled. Sanballat, Tobiah, and Geshem were professional distracters. In Nehemiah 6:2, Nehemiah said, *"Sanballat and Geshem sent me this message: 'Come, let us meet together in one of the villages on the plain of Ono.' But they were scheming to harm me."* Ono seems like the perfect name for this situation. I imagine that's exactly what Nehemiah was thinking: "Oh, no." These men were saying, "Let's meet and discuss what you're doing," when, in reality, they wanted to have a council with him in order to trap him and stop the work.

Choose to live well.

In verse three, Nehemiah said, *"So I sent messengers to them with this reply: 'I am carrying on a great project and cannot go down. Why should the work stop while I leave it and go down to you?'"* Nehemiah was saying, "Look, if I do what you want me to do, I will be distracted from what I have purposed to do." He refused to come down from the wall, and his enemies were thwarted. That's what I call a man who had his priorities set.

Make Your Life Count

If you are afraid to take decisive action to move toward your vision, consider this: It is better to make a decision that will prove to be wrong, but which you can learn from, than not to make any decision at all and never learn anything. Someone has said, "I'd rather try and fail than never try and never know I could succeed." People who succeed *try*. People who don't try have no chance of success.

Your destination is so perfect for you that God doesn't want you to end up anywhere else. He wants you to find your vision and purpose and stay focused on it. If you have gotten off track in life, it doesn't matter how young or old you are: Refocus on your vision and make decisions that will lead you there. Say to

God, "I know I haven't made the best use of my time, gifts, and resources in the past, but I'm going to make the rest of my life count."

Action Steps to Fulfilling Vision

- Write out priorities in each area of your life in relation to your vision.

- What things do you need to eliminate from your life in order to focus on your dream?

- Write out your answers to the discipline questions on pages 145–46. Add any other categories that apply.

Chapter Principles

1. If you want to be successful, you must set priorities for yourself in relation to your vision.

2. Understanding priority will help you accomplish your dream because priority is the key to effective decision-making.

3. You can tell the kind of life you're going to have in the future by the decisions you are making today.

4. *Yes* and *no* are the most powerful words you will ever say. God wants you to be able to say them with precision because they will determine your destiny.

5. When people don't succeed in their visions, it is often because they don't understand that prioritizing creates useful limits on their choices.

6. You have to determine what is beneficial, and you have to define what is beneficial based on the needs of your vision.

7. The only things that should master you are the things that will take you to your goal.

8. Once you are certain of where you are meant to go in life and have truly committed to it, then many extraneous things in your life will fall away on their own.

9. The vision itself decides what is good for you. You don't just do good things. You do things that are good for your vision.

10. Your greatest challenge is not in choosing between good or bad but between *good* and *best*.

11. We end up where we don't really want to be when we take our eyes off the mark.

12. Vision protects you from trying to do everything.

13. When you see your destination, it helps you to discipline your life in ways that train, prepare, and provide for your vision.

14. You will never be disciplined in your life until you have real vision.

Chapter Eleven
Principle #8: Recognize People's Influence on Vision

WHEN YOU BEGIN TO ACT ON YOUR VISION, IT WILL STIR UP BOTH THOSE WHO WANT TO HELP YOU AND THOSE WHO WANT TO HINDER YOU.

Principle number eight is that we must recognize people's influence on our visions. We need other people if we are going to be successful in life because, as I emphasized earlier, we were not created to fulfill our visions alone. As a matter of fact, God specifically said about His first human creation, *"It is not good for the man to be alone"* (Genesis 2:18). We need people to make it in life. Again, individual purpose is always fulfilled within a larger or corporate purpose. Therefore, it's important that we work with others in making our visions a reality.

Remember that Nehemiah reported, *"Then I said to* [the Jews, priests, nobles, officials, and others], *'You see the trouble we are in: Jerusalem lies in ruins, and its gates have been burned with fire. Come, let us rebuild the wall of Jerusalem, and we will no longer be in disgrace'"* (Nehemiah 2:17, emphasis added). Nehemiah was the one who had received the vision, but he had to go to other people to help him get it done. For any vision that you have, God has people prepared to work with you, and they will be a blessing to you.

There will always be a need for positive people in your life. When I went to college, I had a dream to get my degree, and there were people who already had been set apart to help me get through it. Some of them helped me academically, others financially, others with encouragement in my spiritual walk. When you have a dream, that's the way it works. People will always be there, waiting to help you. Therefore, if you have no dream, or if you do not begin to act on it, the people who are supposed to help you won't know where to find you.

You become like those with whom you spend time.

The principle of influence has a twofold application, however, because people can have a negative effect on us as well as a positive one. When you begin to act on your vision, it will stir up both those who want to help you and those who want to hinder you.

The Law of Association

The law of association states that you become like those with whom you spend time. We often underestimate others' influence in our lives. **There are two words that most accurately describe influence:** *powerful* **and** *subtle*. Often, you don't know you're being influenced until it is too late. Whether you realize it or not, however, the influence of those you spend time with has a powerful effect on how you will end up in life, on whether you will succeed or fail.

What we call peer pressure is simply this: people with whom we associate exercising their influence on us, trying to direct our lives in the way they want them to go. We should stop telling young people that they alone have peer pressure. Adults have it, too. They find it hard to disregard other people's opinions. There are people who are sixty, seventy, and eighty years old who give in to peer pressure; almost everyone is affected by it.

You must be careful whom you allow to influence you because your vision will be either encouraged or destroyed by others. There are two kinds of people in this world: those who are with you and those who are against you. I have learned that **people have the potential to create your environment. Your environment then determines your mind-set, and your mind-set determines your future.** Therefore, you must choose your friends wisely, selecting those who are with you and not against you. Show me your friends, and I'll show you your future.

Questions of Influence

You should generally choose friends who are going in the same direction you are and who want to obtain the same things you do, so you can reinforce one another. In light of this truth, I want you to ask yourself three questions. First, "With whom am I spending time?" Who are your closest friends; who are the people you are confiding in?

Choose friends who are going in the same direction as you.

Second, "What are these people doing to me?" In other words, what do they have you listening to, reading, thinking, doing? Where do they have you going? What do they have you saying? How do they have you feeling? What do they have you settling for? That last one is an important one, because your friends can make you comfortable in your misery. Most important, what is being around these people causing you to become? Solomon said, *"He who walks with the wise grows wise, but a companion of fools suffers harm"* (Proverbs 13:20). The *New King James Version* reads, *"The companion of fools will be destroyed."* My version of this maxim is, "If you want to be a success, don't keep company with those who aren't going anywhere in life."

For example, if you associate with people who spend more money than they make, the chances are high that you also will spend more than you make. A friend may say, "That new dress came in, and that's the latest style. You should get it," when you know you can't afford it. When she says, "I have mine; do you have yours yet?" you really feel pressured. Another friend may say, "I traded my car in for a brand new one. You should do the same thing. You have to look right, you know." The result is that you're knocked right off your goals—your payments are so high that you can't save money anymore. Don't let anyone throw you off course any longer. Decide for yourself, "What are my goals and plans?" and don't let others influence you to deny them.

Third, ask yourself, "Is what other people are doing to me a good thing in relation to my vision?" When you start telling people where you're going to go and what you're going to do, they may (even unconsciously) begin to say things to try to hinder your dream.

You need to ask and answer these three questions for your-self truthfully—and regularly—as you progress toward your vision.

Vision Wakes Up Opposition

Nehemiah 4:1 says, *"When Sanballat heard that we were rebuilding the wall, he became angry and was greatly incensed."* People of vision have found that the minute they decide to ful-fill their dreams, all their enemies seem to wake up. Again, as long as you're not doing anything about your vision, no one will bother you. If you start to move toward your vision, however, opposition arises.

For example, suppose you have been a secretary for twenty years, and everybody thinks you're content in your job. One day you decide, "I'm going back to school." When your friends ask you why, you say, "I'm going to get a master's degree in computer science because I want to head a computer company someday." Suddenly, your friends seem to become your enemies. They ask, "Who do you think you are?" or "Do you know how old you are?" or "Do you realize your brain can't handle studying anymore?" or "Who do you think will become your clients?" By the time they finish, you feel like settling down and becoming a secretary again.

It is an interesting phenomenon that certain people will become angry when you step out and start to do something that they have never done. Friends and associates don't want you to break out of your situation because they don't want you to leave them behind. You need to get used to the idea that people may gossip about you and treat you with malice because of your vision. It's all part of the process! It is often proof that you're really doing something with your life.

Opposition often proves you are doing something significant with your life.

Napoleon Hill wrote a great book called *Think and Grow Rich*. From the title, some people might not think this is an appropriate book for believers to read, but it actually contains many of the principles of the Word of God. Hill made a statement that has really stuck with me:

> The majority of people permit relatives, friends, and the public at large to so influence them that they cannot live their own lives, because they fear criticism....Countless numbers of men and women, both young and old, permit relatives to wreck their lives in the name of duty, because they fear criticism.*

That is a powerful statement. Sad to say, sometimes the people who are the most detrimental to the fulfillment of your vision are members of your own family. Some family members may be extremely supportive, but others may not be. This is because they have lived with you for such a long time that they think they know who you are, so they try to talk you out of all your dreams. Your mother may say, "You'd better stay at your job.

---

* Napoleon Hill, *Think and Grow Rich* (New York: Fawcett Crest, 1960), 139.

It's secure, and it has benefits." Your cousin may say, "What are you leaving your job for? That's good money." These are forms of attacks on your vision, even if they are well-intentioned. By the time your family has finished telling you all the reasons you shouldn't follow your dreams, you want to give up on them. In your heart, however, you still have the desire to fulfill them, so you end up frustrated and suffering from things such as high blood pressure.

> ## People who change the world have declared independence from other people's expectations.

The potential for negative influences from family members in regard to vision is probably the reason why the Lord told Abraham, *"Leave your country, your people and your father's household and go to the land I will show you"* (Genesis 12:1). The Scripture doesn't say that Abraham's wife was present at the time, which was probably a good thing. Remember that, later on, Sarah laughed with unbelief when God said she would have a child. (See Genesis 18:1–15.) Joseph also had to leave his family before he could become what was essentially prime minister of Egypt.

Sometimes, we need to pull away from the influence of even those we love if we're going to follow our God-given visions. Many people want you to be what they want you to be, not what you were born to be, and often they end up limiting you. For example, a family member may say, "I know you—you're just like your mother. She never had any business sense. What do you mean you're going to open a store?"

When you step outside what others expect you to be, they begin to see you as a problem. However, people who change the world have declared independence from other people's expectations. That's what makes them successful. Even if people lie about you or start rumors about you, keep your eyes on the mark, continue working, and keep on building. Your passion has to be more powerful than the opposition of those around you. You must be clear about what you're going to do and persevere in doing it.

156

Nehemiah faced this very situation. In Nehemiah 4:2, we read,

> And in the presence of his associates and the army of Samaria, [Sanballat] said, "What are those feeble Jews doing? Will they restore their wall? Will they offer sacrifices? Will they finish in a day? Can they bring the stones back to life from those heaps of rubble?"

Look at the questions Sanballat was asking. When people are angry, they ask questions to discourage you. Verse three says, "*Tobiah the Ammonite, who was at his side, said, 'What they are building—if even a fox climbed up on it, he would break down their wall of stones!'*" In other words, "Don't worry about them. This isn't going to work. It will soon come to nothing." Have you ever heard that before? "Oh, don't worry about that new business. It will last only a couple of months before it folds." That attitude is what I call the "Tobiah Syndrome." When someone says something like that to you, just keep moving forward with your vision.

Don't sacrifice your dreams because of a fear of conflict or disagreement.

The reason some people may begin to hate you when you pursue your vision is that you are exposing their own lack of vision. There are toxic people in the world, and they will pollute your whole life if you let them. They will tell you things such as the following: "You can't do that." "You don't have enough education." "You're too young." "You're too old." "You don't have the right background." "You don't have the right connections." They continually talk in this way. My response to such people is this (essentially): "Leave me alone. I was born into my family, and I didn't choose my brothers and sisters. However, I can choose my friends."

In addressing the problems that come with the law of association, I have had to learn to do three things to protect my vision. The first is disassociation.

Disassociation

Priority requires that there are people and places that you are going to have to disassociate yourself from if you're going to make it to your dream. This fact shouldn't be taken lightly. Some people say that it doesn't really matter with whom they associate, that they wouldn't want to hurt anybody by disassociating from them. Yet Jesus said, *"If the blind leads the blind, both will fall into a ditch"* (Matthew 15:14 NKJV). He was telling us not to be foolish by following those who are spiritually blind. You have to disassociate yourself from people who aren't going anywhere and don't want to go anywhere in life. The sad thing is that some people literally sacrifice their dreams and their lives because they are afraid of having conflict and disagreement with others.

Young people, tell your former companions, "I don't do that any longer. I don't want you coming here. We aren't going in the same direction anymore." Choose the people in your life carefully. There are many people I went to school with that I can't spend time with today. There are people I associated with five years ago that I can't be around any longer. You can outgrow your friends. When you start pursuing God's vision for your life, sometimes you have to change who your close friends are because you're not speaking the same language anymore. Choose people who want you to go where you want to go. Let them be your encouragement.

Don't be afraid to disassociate yourself from people who aren't right for you. Disassociation does not need to be confrontational. Sometimes, you can ease out of people's lives very quietly and very subtly, just as you eased into them. For example—

"I haven't seen you for three weeks."

"Yeah, I've been real busy."

"I haven't seen you for two months."

"Yeah, I've been working on some projects."

"I haven't seen you for a whole year!"

"Yeah, I've really been doing some things!"

Disassociation is not an easy action to take, but it is a very important priority in life. I want to conclude this section by saying that, if you listen to the critics, you won't do what you were born to do. You must ignore the critics and keep on acting in accordance with your vision. Critics criticize because they have too much time on their hands. You need to be so busy that you don't have time to criticize anybody or time to listen to anybody criticizing you. Remember what Nehemiah said when his enemies tried to distract him from his vision: *"I am carrying on a great project and cannot go down. Why should the work stop while I leave it and go down to you?"* (Nehemiah 6:3).

Make sure your potential spouse supports your life goals.

I was talking to a woman one time who was in the midst of a divorce. Her husband didn't really want the divorce, but she had some friends who had gone through divorces, and they were trying to talk her into it. She came to see me and said, "I need to decide whether I should go back to my husband, and I was told you could help me." After I had listened to what she had to say, I told her, "I'll tell you what. Your husband is your best company, because he wants the marriage. Your friends are not really your friends. If you want to save your marriage, don't speak to them any longer. All of them are divorced. That is why they are giving you this advice."

When you're going through an emotionally painful situation, you must be especially careful from whom you receive counsel. You don't want to talk to someone who is still down at the bottom. You want someone who can help you out. When you need help, you don't go to a drowning man.

Limited Association

The second thing I have learned is limited association. You may not want to completely disassociate yourself from some of the people in your life. It is important, however, that you thoughtfully and prayerfully determine how much time you will spend with them. Perhaps **there are some people you will just want to be acquainted with, so that you can back off and leave them alone again if you see that being with them causes your vision to falter.**

Spend major time with positive influence and minor time with negative influence.

For those of you who are dating and becoming excited about your relationships, please take this to heart: When you have a goal for your life, make sure that the person you are interested in is also interested in your goals. Many people get married and then tell their spouses their goals. Often, their spouses say, "I really don't want that." The Bible asks us, *"Can two walk together, unless they are agreed?"* (Amos 3:3 NKJV). Jesus reinforced this theme when He said, *"A house divided against itself will fall"* (Luke 11:17). You don't want to be in a house that is divided. That's what causes confrontation. You want to be in a house with one vision.

It's all right to have casual friends as long as you give them casual time. You don't want to spend quality time with casual friends. It's all right to spend two hours with some people but not two days. It's all right to spend two minutes with some people but not two hours. It depends on the person and his influence on you. In fact, there are some people I can't be around for even two minutes because they're always complaining. Before I talk to them, I am upbeat and ready to give my full energy to life; after I talk to them for two minutes, however, I'm depressed.

You must protect your mental environment. Here's how to do so: Spend major time with positive influence and minor time with negative influence. Stay away from bad situations. Paul quoted the adage, *"Bad company corrupts good character"* (1 Corinthians 15:33). He was telling us, "Choose your company well."

You should also be careful about what you receive from other people in terms of your life's purpose. I have mentioned this before, but I want to mention it again: No one should prophesy anything over you that you weren't already thinking about because God will confirm your vision to you first. Prophecy is for confirmation, exhortation, and encouragement, not for direction. The reason why so many people are confused is that they don't have a vision for their lives yet, and they keep running to various meetings looking for someone to give them a word of prophecy. There are some people who have no self-control. They follow whatever others speak into their lives, and it messes them up, like the friend I mentioned earlier who moved away from his family. This happened because he had no clear vision for his own life. Again, don't allow other people to give you your vision; allow them only to confirm the vision that God has already given to you.

Expanded Association

Third—and this is the most positive of the three—expand your association. If you're going to be successful, you have to spend more time with the right people: people who have the same philosophy and discipline that you do, people who exhibit the kind of character that you want to have. Those are the people with whom you want to expand your relationships. Ask yourself these questions: Who can help me toward my goal? What person can I get close to and learn from?

Spend time with people of vision. When the angel Gabriel announced to Mary that she would become pregnant with Jesus, Mary asked, "How can I have a baby?" God's answer through Gabriel was that this would occur through the power

161

of the Holy Spirit. Yet notice what else the angel said. He mentioned that Elizabeth was pregnant with John the Baptist after she had been both barren and past the age of child-bearing. It was as if God was saying, "Mary, to help you stay strong during this time, you need the faith-inspiring testimony of Elizabeth. She has her own miracle baby, and she's six months ahead of you." The Bible says that Mary went straight to Elizabeth's house and stayed with her for three months. (See Luke 1:26–56.)

Get to know those whom you want to emulate.

God doesn't want you to spend time listening to critics because they will talk you out of your "baby." He wants you to be encouraged by someone who has already been through the morning sickness, so to speak, because there will be times when you'll feel like giving up. During those hard times, that person can tell you, "Honey, you're going to get through it. Don't give up on your dream."

Remember what Jesus did when He wanted to raise a little girl from death? The girl's house was full of people who were crying and moaning, "Oh, she's dead!" They were playing funeral music and were dressed in black. They were beating their chests, tearing their clothes, and throwing ashes on themselves. Everybody was so dark and depressing. It was a pity party. When Jesus arrived, He said to the father, "Put all of them out for Me, please." Jesus wanted an atmosphere of faith, not unbelief. Then He took the girl's parents, along with Peter, James, and John, into the room where she was, and raised her from the dead. (See Mark 5:35–43.)

Accentuate the Positive

We all need other people to guide, help, and encourage us along the path to fulfilling our visions. Because we need the influence of others, however, we are also in danger of the negative effects they may have on us if we—or they—are not careful.

Therefore, it is crucial for us to guard our hearts, thoughts, attitudes, and ideas from being sabotaged by those around us. We must increase the positive influences in our lives and decrease the negative ones as we pursue our individual goals in tandem with others.

Action Steps to Fulfilling Vision

- Answer the three questions posed in the chapter:

  1. *With whom am I spending time?* Who are my closest friends; who are the people I am confiding in?

  2. *What are these people doing to me?* In other words, what do they have you listening to, reading, thinking, doing? Where do they have you going? What do they have you saying? How do they have you feeling? What do they have you settling for?

  3. *Is what these people are doing to me a good thing in light of my vision?*

- Ask yourself: Who can help me toward my goal? What person can I get close to and learn from?

Chapter Principles

1. When you begin to act on your vision, it will stir up both those who want to help you and those who want to hinder you.

2. The law of association states that you become like those with whom you spend time.

3. There are two words that most accurately describe influence: *powerful* and *subtle*.

4. People have the potential to create your environment. Your environment then determines your mind-set, and your mind-set determines your future.

5. People of vision have found that the minute they decide to fulfill their dream, all their enemies seem to wake up.

6. Sometimes, the people who are the most detrimental to the fulfillment of your vision are members of your own family.

7. People who change the world have declared independence from other people's expectations.

8. Three things that will protect your vision are disassociation, limited association, and expanded association.

9. We must increase the positive influences in our lives and decrease the negative ones as we pursue our individual goals in tandem with others.

Chapter Twelve
Principle #9:
Employ the Provision
of Vision

GOD DESIGNED EVERY PURPOSE WITH ITS OWN PROSPERITY.

Principle number nine is that we must understand the power of provision. People often stop dreaming about what they really want to do in life because they know they have few resources with which to do it. They believe they have to pay for their visions with their present incomes when they can barely make ends meet as it is. Similarly, when young people tell their parents what they dream of becoming, the parents often become nervous because they feel their children's dreams are too big for them to finance.

Whatever God Purposes, He Provides For

If we believe that we have to use our own resources to accomplish God-given visions, then we are small dreamers. I want to encourage you that the Bible is very clear concerning the dreams and plans that are in our hearts and how they are meant to be provided for. Proverbs 16:1 says, *"To man belong the plans of the heart, but from the LORD comes the reply of the tongue."* This statement has to do with provision. Whenever a person receives a dream from God, it usually seems impossible. Yet God knows that our provisions are never equal to our visions at the moment we receive them. He realizes that we cannot explain

165

to others—or even ourselves—how we are going to accomplish our visions without the necessary money, people, facilities, or equipment. He knows that often our dreams are big and our bank accounts are small. What is His solution for us? He says that He will give the answer or *"reply of the tongue."*

Our provisions are never equal to our visions at the moment we receive them.

God's will for our lives comes from His own will. That's why He says **it is our job to understand, believe, and write down our visions while it is His responsibility to explain how He's going to accomplish them in His own time.** That frees us to be creative and productive in pursuing our visions. Therefore, if people ask you how you are going to accomplish your dream, you don't have to try to give them a full answer. Tell them you are trusting God for provision each step of the way. Then let God explain to them how it is going to be done. Purpose is your responsibility. Provision is God's responsibility.

Vision and Provision Go Together

Perhaps your dreams are so big they almost frighten you. You don't see how they could ever come to pass. Let me assure you that your initial apprehension is normal. **God often gives us dreams that confound us at first because He wants to make sure we don't attempt to fulfill them apart from Him.** If we try to do so, we won't succeed, because the resources won't be available.

Many people who are doing something significant for God in the world are doing it without their own resources because God doesn't want us to depend on our own abilities. Instead, He wants us to be obedient by putting the vision on paper and then looking to Him to generate the funds and other resources that are needed to support His own work.

Rest assured that God will never give you a vision without provision. The ability and resources are available for whatever you were born to do. Your provision, however, is usually hidden until you act on your vision. Whatever you were born to do attracts what you need to do it. Therefore, you first have to establish what you want to do, and begin to do it, before the need can be met. Most of us work in reverse. We like to see the provisions before we start, but faith doesn't work that way. When we take action, *then* God manifests the provision.

I want to show you proof that everything you need has been provided for you already. Ephesians 1:3 says, *"Praise be to the God and Father of our Lord Jesus Christ, who has* [already] *blessed us in the heavenly realms with **every** spiritual blessing in Christ"* (emphasis added). **God has already blessed you with everything you need.** Where is it? It is in the heavenly realms, the spiritual world. Verse four starts out with the word *"For...."* When we see that word, we understand that, because of the truth of verse four, verse three is a reality: *"For he chose us in him before the creation of the world."*

Your provision is usually hidden until you act on your vision.

God already prepared everything you would need before He created you so that you could do what you were born to do. He knew what you needed because He chose you for your vision a long time ago. God tells us we don't have to worry about our provision because He has already blessed us with every spiritual blessing in the heavenly places. Worry is the greatest sign of doubt in God. If He can put Pharaoh's money into the pockets of the Israelites and take His people into the wilderness loaded down with the gold of the enemy, do you think He can't provide for your needs?

Misconceptions of Prosperity

Prosperity as Excess

One of the reasons we have trouble understanding how God will provide for our visions is that we have a false view of prosperity. We think prosperity means excess, and that is why we worry when we don't already have money in the bank to fund our visions.

Further, our concept of prosperity is more like hoarding. In the Bible, hoarding is referred to as gluttony. A person can be gluttonous even when he has no money or food. Gluttony is a state of mind in which a person never feels he has enough to satisfy him.

Whatever you hoard will begin to destroy you. When we eat more than we need, it becomes a problem called excess weight. That weight causes pressure on the heart. Our arteries begin to clog up, putting us in danger of stroke, all because we loaded up on excess food.

The Bible says that people who have excess money have many burdens, worry, and headaches trying to figure out what to do with their riches and how to protect them. (See, for example, Luke 12:16–21; James 5:1–5.) Too much wealth can cause oppression and even depression. Some people have so many gems and diamonds that they put bars on their windows to protect themselves against theft. They worry every night that someone might break in and take their twenty-thousand-dollar watch, which they rarely wear anyway.

To me, that approach to wealth is foolishness because the riches are a burden rather than a blessing. You don't have to own extravagant things just because you are wealthy. You'd be better off buying a twenty-dollar watch and enjoying your life. That way, if someone takes it, you can just buy another one. All you need to know is the time. You don't have to worry about who is keeping it for you.

Prosperity as Future Needs Met Today

Other people have the idea that prosperity means all our needs should be provided for well ahead of time.

Jesus addressed this misconception when He told His disciples,

Therefore I tell you, do not worry about your life, what you will eat or drink; or about your body, what you will wear. Is

not life more important than food, and the body more impor-
tant than clothes?...So do not worry, saying, "What shall we
eat?" or "What shall we drink?" or "What shall we wear?"
For the pagans run after all these things, and your heavenly
Father knows that you need them. But seek first his kingdom
and his righteousness, and all these things will be given to you
as well.   (Matthew 6:25, 31–33)

Do people worry about something they already have? No. Worry isn't related to our present supply. It is related to a perceived or potential lack in the future. Jesus was asking His disciples, in effect, "Why do you want something that you don't need right now? You are focusing on the wrong thing. Seek first God's kingdom and His righteousness, and these things will come with the job. Don't pursue them; they will follow you."

Prosperity doesn't mean tomorrow's need is met today, but that today's need is met today.

Jesus concluded His statements on provision by saying, *"Tomorrow will worry about itself. Each day has enough trouble of its own"* (v. 34). I interpret this to mean, "If you have something right now, then enjoy it." In other words, if the rent on the house is paid, then enjoy the house for the month. Stop worrying about the next month that isn't even here yet! Live in your house, sleep in your bed, cook in your kitchen, relax in your living room. Have joy in the house that is paid for today. We get ulcers over how we are going to pay for next month's provision because we don't allow ourselves to live in the present.

Prosperity doesn't mean that tomorrow's need is met today; it means that today's need is met today. We find the same concept in the Lord's Prayer: *"Give us today our daily bread"* (v. 11). Jesus tells us not to worry about tomorrow because it has its own supply (v. 34), and tomorrow we may need even more than we do today. When we get to tomorrow, the supply will be there. We must understand what prosperity really is in order to grasp the foundational principle of how God provides for our visions.

The Nature of Real Prosperity

One of the Hebrew words that is translated *"prosperity"* in the Bible is *shalev* (see, for example, Psalm 30:6; Psalm 73:3), which means "tranquil," "being at ease," "peaceable," and "quietness." Another Hebrew word for prosperity is *shalom* (see Psalm 35:27; Jeremiah 33:9), which means "peace," "safe," "well," "happy," and "health." The Bible is saying that prosperity is peace. Prosperity is also harmony. When things are in balance, we say they are peaceful. **True prosperity means to be free of worry and fear and reflects a state of contentedness that everything necessary is being taken care of.**

God provides for the birds, but He doesn't hand-deliver food to their nests.

Jesus used an analogy from nature to help explain prosperity: *"Look at the birds of the air; they do not sow or reap or store away in barns, and yet your heavenly Father feeds them. Are you not much more valuable than they? Who of you by worrying can add a single hour to his life?"* (Matthew 6:26–27).

Some people interpret this passage to mean that, since God is supposed to take care of them, they don't need to do anything themselves. They're going to just sit back and let the Lord bless them. If they need anything, they will pray, and someone will bring groceries to their front doors or pay for the gasoline in their cars or give them several hundred dollars. Therefore, they just wait for God to act.

However, let's look at the implication of the passage. How does God feed birds? He provides for them, but He doesn't personally hand-deliver food to their nests! The birds don't just sit around and wait for God to stop by with their meals. When Jesus said the heavenly Father feeds the birds, He meant that

170

everything they need has been made available for them, but they have to go and get it.

God does not build a bird's nest. He provides the twigs. The bird has to find them, pick them up, and bring them back to the tree it has chosen for a home. God does not leave worms on the top of the ground every morning. The bird has to go digging for them. It has to keep working, working, working until it finishes building its nest. It has to keep working, working, working until it gets the worm.

Whatever God Calls For, He Provides For

A principle we talked about earlier applies here: Whatever God calls for, He provides for. God provides us with what we need, though usually not directly. If you are a college student, your parents may provide your tuition to go to school, but they cannot make you learn. The provision is made, but the work is up to you. Your parents cook food and put it on the table for you, but you have to eat it; you have to get the energy from it yourself. It's the same way with God. He provides, but He doesn't do the work for us. We have to go after what God has provided as our supply.

Every Purpose Has Its Own Prosperity

Another fundamental aspect of provision is that God has designed every purpose with its own prosperity. Your purpose has built-in provision for it. God never requires from you what He does not already have in reserve for you.

Here is the key: Your prosperity is directly related to your purpose in life. The nature and degree of your prosperity is determined by what your assignment is. You were not born to have too much or too little. You were born to fulfill God's purpose. When you capture your vision—the part you're supposed to contribute to your generation and succeeding generations, the role you're supposed to play in history—when you capture that and are doing it, you will see that all your provisions are automatically built into it.

In this way, you don't ultimately work for money or food, because you're too busy living. You were not created by God just to pay a mortgage. You were not given life simply to keep food in the refrigerator. In your heart, you know that's true. If this is what you're doing, you are probably frustrated with your situation. By the time you turn sixty, you will look back at your life and say, "Did I enjoy any of this?" Perhaps you have a nice home, but you are there only between 9 P.M. and 6 A.M. The rest of the time, you're helping someone else get rich, and that person is at home playing golf behind his house and enjoying the company of his family and friends while you are busy at work.

Your purpose has built-in provision for it.

You and I have prosperity based on our assignments, not on keeping up with the Joneses. We should get rid of whatever is excess in our lives. We are as rich as our purposes, and our visions aren't yet completed. We still have provision coming to us that no one can hold back.

Sometimes, God doesn't give us all the resources we need to fulfill our visions because He has called other people to provide them for us. God may have provisions all over the world waiting for you. He may move you a thousand miles to get you where you were meant to be, to do things you were born to do, to fulfill the purpose in your own heart while, at the same time, fulfilling the purpose in His heart.

Therefore, if you want to go to college, don't abandon your dream just because your mother doesn't have the money for it. Your mother doesn't need to pay your bills. Your heavenly Father has promised to do that. Mary and Joseph's money came from wise men on camels. When they said yes to God's vision, the wise men traveled a great distance to get to them. God will supply your provision, even if He has to have someone cross the desert to get it to you. God has provision for you that no one but He knows about.

Therefore, you have all the provisions you need for your vision, including your finances, staff, buildings, and anything else that is required. There are people who were born to help you fulfill your vision. There are people who went to school to learn a skill just to work for you. Right now, they're in a pre-occupation job because you haven't started your business yet. All the resources you need are already in place; they will become visible in God's timing once you start pursuing your vision.

Provision Is Right for the Vision

God is a God of provision. He is Jehovah-Jireh, "The Lord Will Provide." He provides everything, but He provides it after you begin the work of the vision. **Your obedience to your vision affects not only your life but also the lives of those who will work with you.** This means that obedience to vision is not a private issue. It affects everyone who is supposed to work with you and be impacted by your life.

Prosperity means having everything that is needed. It doesn't necessarily mean having a large bank account, several cars, and a large house, although you might need those things to fulfill your vision. For example, because of our purpose, my wife and I need a long dining room table that can seat a large number of people since we often have guests of the ministry to dinner. That's part of our assignment. It might also be yours, depending on what you are called to do. However, perhaps you need a four-chair table rather than a twelve-chair table because you usually just have your family at dinner. Instead of using the money on a large table, you use it for other things related to your personal or church vision. Similarly, I may not need something that you must have to fulfill your purpose. If I had it, it would be excess. The point is that God provides for all the needs of our visions, no matter what they are, large or small.

Use Your Provision

Several years ago, when I was visiting a friend in Detroit, I said, "You know, I've always wanted to tour the Ford Motor

173

Company. I've heard a lot about Mr. Ford and the way they make cars there, and I'd like to see it for myself." We ended up spending a whole afternoon there. The man conducting the tour showed us some massive buildings, including the corporate office and the place where they design the cars.

Then he took us to look at another big building and said, "This is where we do all the production work on the parts." We went through what looked like one massive building, but there were smaller storehouses within it. Every section had a different name, and there were millions of parts stored in each section. I pointed to one section and asked the guide, "What is this?" and he said, "These are the cars we're preparing for 2005." I said, "Wait a minute; it's only 1998." He said, "Yeah, but we are at least five years ahead. This one is for 2002, this is for 2003, this is for 2004, and this one is for 2005." When I asked if I could see the cars, he said, "No, the cars themselves are not yet made. We make the parts first. However, these are not the parts we will use on the new cars. These are the replacement parts in case any repairs would be needed."

Clean out your heavenly warehouse.

The company makes the spare parts before they build the new cars. Then they make the cars. That's why, when anything needs to be replaced on your car, the part is already prepared. They prepare what you're going to need before you even buy your car.

As I listened to our guide explain this, I felt as if the Holy Spirit was speaking to me right in that warehouse. He said, "That's exactly the meaning of Ephesians 1:3: *'Praise be to the God and Father of our Lord Jesus Christ, who has blessed us in the heavenly realms with every spiritual blessing in Christ.'* Everything you're going to need for your vision is already provided for. I have it all reserved in big storehouses in heaven. Even before you came on the scene, I had it all prepared."

My good friend Jesse Duplantis once told me about an unusual experience he had. He had a spiritual vision in which Jesus took him on a tour of heaven. He has written about this experience in a book. At one point, Jesus and he came to a large area of heaven where there were big, massive warehouses. There were names on the warehouses, and he saw one with his name on it, so he asked Jesus, "What's in that warehouse?" Jesus said, "Do you want to see?" He said, "Sure. My name is there." They went up to the warehouse and opened its large door. Inside, piled up to the ceiling, was what looked like billions of dollars' worth of things. In the corner was a small, empty space. He asked, "Lord, the whole place is filled with all these magnificent things, but what's that empty spot right there by the door?" Jesus said, "That's all you've asked for so far."

God is not short of anything you need.

After he told me that story, I said to myself, "I'm going to die empty. I'm going to clean out my warehouse before I leave planet earth." When we go to heaven, most of us are going to be shocked at what was ours for use on earth that we never asked for. We must use what is in our warehouses. Daily, we should ask God, "Deliver to me what I need today." Second Peter 1:3 says that God's *"divine power has given us everything we need for life and godliness."* Where is it? It's waiting for you to ask for it with confidence. God is not short of anything you need.

What I'm concerned about is that you may be asking for some things that *aren't* yours. Let me explain. If you pursue the wrong assignment, you're going to need things you can't get, because the provision isn't there unless the vision is yours. It's someone else's assignment, and he has his own warehouse. Sometimes, people make demands on God that He can't supply because He can't give us what doesn't belong to us. Again, knowing God's will for your life is the key to your prosperity.

Five Specific Ways God Provides for Vision

I now want to discuss five specific ways that the Scriptures teach us God provides the resources—financial and otherwise—that we need to fulfill the visions He gives us.

Land and Its Inherent Wealth

The first way God provides for our visions is through our ability to obtain and use land and the resources inherent in it. Until you own land, you are still considered somewhat poor, and you are not really secure. As long as you are renting, someone else owns you. Although real estate prices fluctuate, there is a special prosperity in owning land.

Land is God's concept of wealth. Note that the first thing God placed man in was the Garden of Eden, or real estate. Genesis 2:7–12 says,

> The LORD God formed the man from the dust of the ground and breathed into his nostrils the breath of life, and the man became a living being. Now the LORD God had planted a garden in the east, in Eden; and there he put the man he had formed. And the LORD God made all kinds of trees grow out of the ground—trees that were pleasing to the eye and good for food. In the middle of the garden were the tree of life and the tree of the knowledge of good and evil. A river watering the garden flowed from Eden; from there it was separated into four headwaters. The name of the first is the Pishon; it winds through the entire land of Havilah, where there is gold. (The gold of that land is good; aromatic resin and onyx are also there.)

This passage describes the wealth of the land surrounding Eden. God said there's gold, resin, and onyx in the land. Resin is a fragrant gum, similar to the precious substance myrrh. Onyx is a type of gem. All these things are in the land. Note that this passage describes what the world was like before the Fall, when everything was perfect, yet God was talking about gold, aromatic resin, and gems. He was saying, "Adam, there's richness in the land." Not only do you have use of what is on the surface of the land, such as trees and fruit, but you also have use of what is under the ground.

Sometimes, a person has to work hard to get the riches that are within the land. For example, a fruit gatherer doesn't work quite as hard as an oilman does in order to get results. To harvest fruit, he stays on the surface of the earth and picks fruit off trees and plants. However, to drill for oil, a person has to get really dirty. He has to dig deep in the ground. It takes time and pressure. Here's the lesson I think we can draw from this: Those who are willing to work hard, to go the extra mile, are the ones who get deep into wealth.

From time to time, the United States has had to go begging the oil-rich countries, "Please, drop your prices." With all the farms in Kansas and Nebraska and elsewhere, America still needs oil. Why? Oil is needed to run the combines that reap the harvests on the farms. Those whose wealth comes from under the ground seem to rule those who gain their wealth from working on the surface of the earth.

Let's look at another example from Genesis that shows us that wealth is inherent in land. What was God's first promise to Abraham?

> The LORD had said to Abram,...."Go to the land I will show you."...Abram traveled through the land as far as the site of the great tree of Moreh at Shechem. At that time the Canaanites were in the land. The LORD appeared to Abram and said, "To your offspring I will give this land." (Genesis 12:1, 6–7)

God made the same promise of inheritance of land to Abraham's son Isaac (see Genesis 26:2–4) and grandson Jacob (see Genesis 28:10–15). The Lord continually reminded them of the land they were to inherit. God also reaffirmed this promise of land to the Israelites through Moses. (See Exodus 3:7–10, 15–17.)

In Genesis 13:15, God said the land would forever belong to Abraham's descendants. Even today, in the state of Israel, land is leased, rather than sold, to the citizens. No private citizen owns property. A person can build and own a house, but he doesn't own the property upon which it stands. The government owns the land. It is considered God's property and therefore is secured for Him.

The previous government of the Bahamas, under colonialism, was the United Bahamian Party. Overall, they didn't impress me, but they did one thing that impressed me: They were conscious of the value of land. They would lease land to people for up to ninety-nine years, but they still owned it. They said, in effect, "You can make money off the land, but you don't own it." Have you ever wondered why foreign investors want to buy land in your country? Those who own the land are the decision-makers. They are the ones who influence policy and legislation, not those who work for them.

According to the biblical record, therefore, **land seems to be God's first order of prosperity.** I think it's desirable for most people to own land. Young people, if your parents left you land, don't exchange your perpetual inheritance for a pot of soup. (See Genesis 25:29–34.) Live very simply, if you have to, but keep the land because there's wealth in it.

My prayer is that you will truly understand the value of land. My beloved friends, some of us have been so heavenly oriented that we have practically forsaken the earth, which has been given to us by God. Matthew 5:3–12 is called the Beatitudes. I like to call them the "attitudes to be." In other words, these are the attitudes God wants you to have in life. Notice the attitude in verse five: *"Blessed are the meek, for they will inherit...."* What? Heaven? No, according to Jesus, if you're meek, you inherit *"the earth"* (v. 5). Christians always think in terms of heaven because that is where their focus is. Yet God didn't create humanity for heaven—He created us to fulfill His purposes on earth.

Meekness means discipline or self-control. If you control your spending and don't use your money on things that are automatically going to depreciate, and if you cut back on your expenses and start putting your money in the bank, then you can save up a nice down payment for a piece of property. You can own land if you exercise discipline and self-control in your life.

How do you do this in practical terms? Stop buying lunch every day when you can take your lunch to work, and then put that excess money into your savings. Keep your Toyota until you buy your property; then you can buy a Lexus. Put your true priorities ahead of any luxuries and you may be amazed at how much you can save toward your vision's goals.

The Ability to Work

The second thing through which God provides for our visions is our work. When you decide to move forward with your dream, it will often take a great amount of work. I define work as the passion that is generated by a purpose.

Work is passion that is generated by a purpose.

Many people misunderstand the nature of work. I've heard people say, "I'm so mad at Adam. Because Adam sinned, now I have to toil at a job." They don't realize that work was given to humankind before the Fall: *"The LORD God took the man and put him in the Garden of Eden to work it and take care of* ["cultivate" NAS] *it"* (Genesis 2:15). Cultivation involves both creativity and effort. Work is not a curse, but a great blessing. Genesis 1:28 says that God blessed the male and female and gave them dominion over the earth. He blessed them in all their dominion assignments—including work.

The primary reason God gave us work is found in Genesis 2:2–3:

> *By the seventh day God had finished the work he had been doing; so on the seventh day he rested from all his work. And God blessed the seventh day and made it holy, because on it he rested from all the work of creating that he had done.*

God Himself worked when He created the world, and He still works to carry out His purposes. For example, Paul said

179

in Philippians 2:13, *"It is God who works in you to will and to act according to his good purpose."* **Because you are made in God's image and likeness, you are designed to work.** Remember that work is meant to include creativity and cultivation, not drudgery.

Another significant aspect of work is that it reveals your potential. You cannot show what you have inside unless demands are made on it, and demands are placed on it by work.

Moreover, work needs to be kept in its proper place. The Bible says that God worked hard and completed His work, but that He also stopped His work and rested. He didn't work seven days a week just for the sake of working. He stopped when it was appropriate, and He has instructed us to do the same. (See Exodus 20:9–10.)

It is through worship and communion with God that humankind receives vision, vocation, and work. Jesus, the Second Adam, seemed to have two favorite words that reflected God's purposes for humankind. One of those words was *Father.* He was always talking about His Father in heaven and seeking His presence in prayer. The other was *work.* For example, consider these statements of Jesus: *"My food is to do the will of Him who sent Me, and to finish His work"* (John 4:34 NKJV). *"My Father is always at his work to this very day, and I, too, am working"* (John 5:17). *"As long as it is day, we must do the work of him who sent me. Night is coming, when no one can work"* (John 9:4). *"I have brought you glory on earth by completing the work you gave me to do"* (John 17:4).

Jesus was intent on doing His Father's work to completion. We are to aspire to fulfill God's purposes while developing and using the gifts and talents He has given us. We aren't to be lazy; instead, we are to have visions for our lives and to be willing to work so that they can be fulfilled. **Our motivation for work is to complete the purposes for which we were created.**

Jesus said,

> *I tell you the truth, you are looking for me, not because you saw miraculous signs but because you ate the loaves and had your fill. Do not work for food that spoils, but for food that endures to eternal life, which the Son of Man will give you.* (John 6:26–27)

In other words, there's a higher reason to work than simply providing for physical needs. Again, don't work just to pay bills. Don't work only to buy food. Understand the true nature of work. In the Garden, there was no supervisor, no one to hand out paychecks. Work was given to Adam because it was a natural part of his being. Through work, he fulfilled part of his purpose as a human being created in God's image.

Work reveals your potential.

We have been designed to work in such a way that we can fashion things into something more than they were in their original state. We are to multiply or enhance what we have been given. In the parable of the talents, the man traveling out of the country entrusted the first servant with five talents, the second with two, and the third with one. It is implied that the man said to his servants before he left, "Now, when I come back, I don't want to see just the money I gave you. I want to see an increase in my investment." When the man returned, and the servant with the one talent had done nothing to increase his master's money, he was called *"wicked"* and *"lazy"* (Matthew 25:26). If we're still working at the same level we were working at ten years ago and haven't improved at all, there's something wrong.

Isn't it interesting that the harder you work, the "luckier" you get? Sometimes, you hear people say, "You're lucky that you're rich and successful." Unless the person inherited the money, that isn't luck. That's hard work. So if you want to get lucky, start working hard.

Matthew 25:16, which comes from the parable of the talents, is a powerful verse: *"The man who had received the five talents went at once and put his money to work and gained five more."* How did the man gain more money? He put his original money to work, and the money multiplied. God wants us to go to work to multiply His kingdom on earth through our visions.

The Ability to Cultivate

Third, God has given us the ability to cultivate things. *"The LORD God took the man and put him in the Garden of Eden to work it and take care of* [cultivate] *it"* (Genesis 2:15). It is interesting to note that God wanted humankind to manage and nurture the vegetation. God prefers cultivation to barrenness and wilderness, and **He has given us the ability to cultivate as one way of reflecting His image.** Recall that in Genesis 1:2, God created or cultivated the earth out of a *"formless and empty"* state.

The situation with most pieces of property that are currently being developed is that the property had been there a long time, but no one had ever done anything about it. For example, you may have passed by a piece of property every day and never thought much about it until you saw bulldozers and other construction machinery on the premises. A large part of the gift of cultivation is the ability to see potential in what others view as wasteland.

Let me tell you the story of Hog Island in the Bahamas. Years ago, people used to dump garbage on the island, and the wild hogs there used to scavenge through all the mess. It definitely lived up to its name. There were also wild dogs roaming around. No self-respecting person wanted to be seen there.

Then, one day, someone came to the Bahamas, flew over Hog Island, and saw something there that no one else could see. He took Hog Island, cultivated it, and made it productive. Today, Hog Island is a destination for vacationers. It has a new name. It's called *Paradise*. What a change! Can anything good come out of Hog Island? All it takes is someone to manage it.

Suppose someone came to you and said, "Look, there's some land available in our claims in a rural area. Would you be interested in buying it?" You might think that would be a waste of time and money because you would prefer a piece of property downtown. Yet that would show you don't have a vision for the future because downtown is already cultivated. When the man bought Hog Island, he bought it for practically nothing because the seller figured, "Oh, it's just hogs. You can have it." The man who bought it, however, didn't see only hogs. He saw a resort.

Cultivate what is around you and make it a resource for your vision.

You can cultivate what is around you and make it a resource for your vision. That's what we are doing at Bahamas Faith Ministries. We bought a piece of barren land in the center of the island at a very good price, and we are turning it into an international leadership center. God wants people who can dream and then act. Maybe your neighborhood used to be residential, but now it's mainly a business strip. You don't realize the power you have in your house in terms of a business. Dream. Think. Look. Open your eyes. You could move into an apartment for a year, turn your house into a business or restaurant, and then build another nice house out of the proceeds of the business. Cultivate what you own to further your vision.

The Ability to Preserve and Reserve for the Future

Another way God provides for your vision is by giving you wisdom to preserve and reserve for the future. For example, Joseph was sent to Egypt ahead of his brothers and his father Jacob because God knew a famine was coming, and they would need to be preserved. When poverty struck the land, Joseph's family would need a place to go to survive and then prosper when times got better. There are people whom God calls to be planters, and God will send them ahead of you to prepare the way for you.

God will also put things on reservation for you so that, when you need them in the future, they'll be there for you. Don't plan only for today, but also for tomorrow. Don't worry, but plan. In fact, **planning destroys worry.** It's when you *don't* plan that you start worrying. We live on the daily bread God gives us, but He also wants us to plan for things. God will bless you, and He will provide for the vision, if you know how to put things on reservation for the future. For example, God gave Joseph a reservation plan during the famine. He was able to harvest the grain during the seven years of abundance and store it for the years of famine so that Egypt and the surrounding lands would have food when the drought hit.

Don't plan only for today, but also for tomorrow.

God knows the future, and He will give you insight to put things on reserve for times when you will need them. For instance, when you put your money into savings and investments, you put it on reserve while increasing your capital because you know that the needs in your life will change, and you want to be prepared financially for when that time comes. I like what the master in Jesus' parable said about the servant who took the one talent he had been given and buried it in the ground. He said, essentially, "You could at least have taken it out of the ground and put it in the bank and gotten some interest on it." (See Matthew 25:14–27.) God will bless you when you put things on reserve.

The Ability to Pass Along Wealth

Another way God provides for vision is by enabling you to help future generations with their dreams. God doesn't want only you to enjoy the wealth; He wants your children and grandchildren to enjoy it, too. *"A good man leaves an inheritance for his children's children"* (Proverbs 13:22). What about your great-grandchildren? The great-grandchildren of the man who developed Hog Island will inherit "Paradise." What is your vision of inheritance for your descendants?

What is your vision of inheritance for your descendants?

God wants us to think generationally. He is always thinking and speaking in generational terms. Therefore, when He speaks to you, He is also talking of your descendants or the generations that will follow you. God gives wealth in generations, and that is why your planning and reservation for the future must include this consideration, as well.

Action Steps to Fulfilling Vision

- Has your definition of prosperity changed as a result of reading this chapter? Why or why not?

- What resources do you need to fulfill your vision? List them, and then trust God to provide for all the needs of your vision as He has promised to do.

- How will you use the information in this chapter to pursue provision for your vision?

Chapter Principles

1. It is our job to understand, believe, and write down our visions, while it is God's responsibility to accomplish them.

2. God often gives us dreams that initially confound us because He wants to make sure we don't attempt to fulfill them apart from Him.

3. God will never give you a vision without the provision for it.

4. The ability and resources are available for what you were born to do, yet your provision is usually hidden until you act on your vision.

5. God has already blessed us with every spiritual blessing in the heavenly places.

6. Prosperity doesn't mean that tomorrow's need is met today; it means that today's need is met today.

7. True prosperity means to be free of worry and fear. It reflects a state of contentedness that everything necessary is being taken care of.

8. God has designed every purpose with its own prosperity.

9. Sometimes, God doesn't give us all the resources we need to fulfill our visions because He has called other people to provide them for us.

10. Your obedience to your vision affects not only your life, but also the lives of those who will work with you.

11. When we go to heaven, most of us are going to be shocked at what was ours for use on earth that we never asked for.

12. Five specific ways that God provides the resources to fulfill our visions are (1) land and its inherent wealth, (2) the ability to work, (3) the ability to cultivate, (4) the ability to preserve and reserve for the future, and (5) the ability to pass along wealth (generational wealth).

Chapter Thirteen
Principle #10: Use Persistence in Achieving the Vision

EVERY TRUE VISION WILL BE TESTED FOR AUTHENTICITY.

The tenth principle is that we must be persistent if we are going to achieve the visions God has given us. As I wrote earlier, you must realize that obstacles are going to come against you and your vision. Even though God gave the vision, that doesn't mean it's going to be easy to obtain. Please don't think that you are exempt from this reality. Trouble isn't going to say about you, "I guess I'll just leave him alone." When you decide to be somebody, everything is going to try to get in the way of your vision. You must be prepared for the challenges, for they are coming.

Think about it: There's no resistance if you're not moving. People who aren't doing anything have nothing to worry about. If you don't want problems, just don't do anything important in life. However, if you are following your vision and you encounter problems, you can say, "Thank you, Lord; at least I'm moving forward!"

God says that, **even though there will be times of stress, disappointment, and pressure, the vision *will* come to pass.**

It is not a matter of whether it's going to be fulfilled; it's a matter of whether we're going to be true to it in the midst of trials so that God can bring it to pass. One of the words that describes the essence of God's nature is *faithfulness*. This is because He is true to what He has decided to accomplish, and nothing can stop Him. We need to manifest this characteristic in our own lives.

Another word that helps us understand God's nature in relation to persistence in purpose is the word *steadfast*. To be steadfast means to stand fast or stand steady in the face of resistance. If you are steadfast, then, when opposition comes, you don't turn and go back where you were. You push forward. Opposition should strengthen your resolve and revive your stamina.

Let every opposition strengthen you rather than stop you.

Courage is another key word in regard to persistence. It is the ability to stand up in the face of fear. It is impossible, in fact, to have courage *without* fear. In a sense, if we don't have any fear, we're not living in faith. That may sound like a strange statement, yet faith always demands that we do something we know we can't do on our own, and this challenge often causes us to fear at first. God told Joshua, *"Be strong and courageous"* (Joshua 1:6, 9). Why did He say that? Clearly, Joshua must have been scared! Fear, however, is a positive thing when it gives birth to courage. If you're afraid to step out in your vision because it's so big, then let your courage come to life as you trust God. Courage means, "I'm afraid, but I'm still moving." Jesus loves for us to do the impossible because the impossible is always possible with God. (See Matthew 19:26.)

When a person finds his purpose, then, if trouble comes, he can smile and say, "This won't last. With God, I'm tougher than this." When you draw on God's strength, you are tougher than your trials because you see them in a different light. You realize that every resistance to your vision gives you the opportunity to become wiser, not weaker. Let every opposition strengthen you rather than stop you. Paul said that trials refine our faith and make us better. That is why we can say, "Bring on the challenges!"

Overcoming Challenges

There are many types of challenges and pressures in life. During His time on earth, Jesus showed us how to bring a vision to pass in the midst of such challenges. He faced similar problems and obstacles to what you and I face today, yet His vision came to pass. He is our greatest Teacher when it comes to learning how to overcome challenges.

Difficult Family Background

Life is tough even at the start for some of us. Perhaps your parents were divorced when you were just a child. Maybe your father is an alcoholic and your mother is a drug addict. Perhaps you aren't even sure who your father is. Or if you know who he is, you wish you didn't. Jesus knows what it feels like to have a difficult family background, because He was called "illegitimate." He was born under what the world considered "questionable circumstances." (See Matthew 1:18–25.) Yet that did not stop Him from knowing His relationship to His heavenly Father and fulfilling His purpose as God's Son. No matter what your background is, your relationship with your Father in heaven will help you overcome your difficult circumstances and fulfill your purpose as God's child.

Family Expectations

Do you feel pressured by family expectations to pursue a certain career or lifestyle when you know that isn't God's plan for you? You don't always have to wait until you're older or "have it all together" before you know God's will for your life. Perhaps your parents have told you, "You are going to do this," but you feel called to do something else. Jesus faced a similar challenge. When He was twelve, He knew what He was born to do. Yet Jesus' earthly parents didn't understand His vision or why He was pursuing it, even when He said, *"Didn't you know I had to be in my Father's house?"* (Luke 2:49; see verse 50). Then, when Jesus grew older, His mother tried to push Him into fulfilling His vision prematurely, and He had to tell her, *"My time has not yet come"* (John 2:4). Even though Jesus respected and honored His parents (see Luke 2:51–52), He had to follow God's purpose for His life. As difficult as it might be to experience the disapproval of family members, you must follow the vision God has given you. At the same time, you should always show them love and respect.

The Jealousy and Scheming of Others

Jesus went through everything you can imagine. There were people who were against Him, who continually schemed to make Him fail. There were those who liked to set Him up for a fall by asking Him trick questions. A crowd once tried to push Him off a cliff. The religious leaders plotted to kill Him. Do you think people call you names? They called Jesus names, too. They called Him demon-possessed and illegitimate. They said He was a glutton and a drunkard. They hit Him with everything. The harshest taunt and the highest evil, however, was when they said He was full of the devil.

Persistence is the desire to withstand every opposition.

How did Jesus overcome? How did He succeed in His vision? How did He finish the work the Father had sent Him to do when He faced all that opposition? Jesus was able to remain composed through all those trials because what He had in His heart was bigger than all their threats, accusations, and insults. He knew how to persevere with a dream. Likewise, **the vision in your heart needs to be larger than any opposition that comes against you so you can persist in your life's purpose.**

Destiny Demands Diligence

Destiny demands diligence. I recommend that you write that statement down on a piece of paper and put it where you can see it every day. If you are going to quit after a couple of fights, you will never win. Persistence is the desire to withstand every opposition. Whenever obstacles come along, persistence responds with attitudes such as these:

"You might as well give up, because I'm not going to stop."

"Get out of my way, because I'm coming through."

"No matter what I lose, I still have me, so I'll be back!"

Persistence says to life what Jacob said to the Lord: *"I will not let you go unless you bless me"* (Genesis 32:26).

Persistent people never take no for an answer when it comes to their visions.

Nehemiah could have stopped his work on the wall of Jerusalem because of all the problems, slander, and jeers, but he was persistent. He was determined to complete his vision. You will never be successful unless you have the spirit of persistence. Persistence means that

- you insist on having what you are going after.
- you stand up against resistance until you wear it down.
- you make people who are against you so tired of fighting that they either become your friends or leave you alone.
- you stop only after you've finished.

How badly do you want your vision? Jesus told a story in Luke 18 about a persistent woman. She tirelessly appealed to the judge with her request for justice until he said, in essence, "Give it to her!" (See Luke 18:2–8.) God wants you to do the same. He wants you to say, "Life, this belongs to me." If Life refuses on Monday, then go back on Tuesday and say, "This belongs to me." If Life says no on Tuesday, then go back on Wednesday and say, "This belongs to me!" If Life says no on Thursday, go back on Friday morning and say the same thing, and so on. Life will eventually say, "Here, take it!" Then you can calmly say, "Thank you very much." Many people lose because they quit when Life says no the first time, but persistent people win. They never take no for an answer when it comes to their visions.

Stay in the Fight

Once, when I was staying at a hotel in Israel, I couldn't sleep because I wasn't yet used to the time difference. At about two in the morning, I was up watching a boxing match on television. It was a twelve-round title match, and the boxer from Mexico was pummeling the boxer from the United States. Every time the American boxer moved forward to fight, the other boxer pounded him.

Fight until you feel the joy of victory.

By the sixth round, the U.S. boxer was getting beaten badly, and at the end of the round, he stumbled back into his corner, sat down on the stool, and sagged as if he were a sack of potatoes. Then I saw something happen. In seconds, several men went to work on him. One grabbed a bucket of water and doused him with it. The next grabbed a soaking-wet sponge and squeezed water all over his face. Another applied ointment to soothe his wounds. These men were all talking to him at once, and they were rubbing him down as they talked. Even though he was getting trounced, they were telling him, "You can do this. You can get back out there. You're strong! You're better than he is!" One of the men said, "Keep your left hook, okay? Keep your left hook. He's a slow left. You can get him with that left." After about two minutes, the boxer jumped up, saying, "Yeah! Oh, yeah!" He ran back out there, and everything changed in the seventh round.

Guess who won the fight? The one who had been about to quit in the sixth round won the fight and received the prize. There was blood everywhere, but under that blood was the champion. When he won the decision, all his strength came back. He ran around the room screaming. When you win, you forget all the pounding you received during the fight.

Sometimes, you will get beaten up pretty badly in life, but stay in the fight. Fight until you feel the joy of victory. When you think you're going to lose, and you stumble back into the corner of life, the Lord will come and pour the cool water of His Word on your head. He will take the ointment of the Holy Spirit and bring healing to your wounds. He will rub life back into your spirit so you can jump back out and say, "Hey! Come on, Life!" Just like the boxer's coaching team, the Holy Spirit speaks good things into your spirit, such as *"Greater is he that is in you, than he that is in the world"* (1 John 4:4 KJV). Life will be tough, but get back out there and start throwing blows. Keep your left up. That's persistence.

The light of God's vision in your heart is stronger and brighter than any darkness in this world.

We know that God wants us to be fighters because the Bible calls us soldiers. (See 2 Timothy 2:3–4.) We are warriors. We are people of battle. The Bible also refers to us as those who *"wrestle"* (Ephesians 6:12 NKJV). This is because we don't just receive medals from God. We earn them. **If God didn't want you to fight, He would have given you the medal without the conflict.**

The Bible says, *"They overcame him by the blood of the Lamb and by the word of their testimony"* (Revelation 12:11). Some people don't have a testimony of overcoming. Their testimony is, "I went through the fire, and I got burned. I went under the water and almost drowned. I have scars in my life! Let me testify about how I've been beaten up." Other people are so spiritually "clean-cut" that you know they have never yet had a scrimmage with the devil. Yet those who have a true testimony usually don't even have to talk about it because it is evident in their lives.

You may have many bumps and bruises, but keep on walking toward your goal, trusting in God. It's going to get tough, but you have what it takes to win because **God has promised that He will stay with you and work out the steps of your plan.** I like what Paul said in Romans 8:

> *Who shall separate us from the love of Christ? Shall trouble or hardship or persecution or famine or nakedness or danger or sword?...No, in all these things we are more than conquerors through Him who loved us* [and called us and gave us our visions].　　　　　　　　　　　　　　　　(vv. 35, 37)

It is those who endure to the end who succeed.

God has put so much in you that if you are willing to capture it, nothing can stop you. There is not enough darkness in the world to extinguish the light God has put within you. The light of God's vision in your heart is so strong and bright that all the darkness of the planet, all the darkness of people's opinions, and all the darkness of past failures can never put it out.

Bear Up under Pressure

Perseverance actually means "to bear up under pressure." I like this quote from Eleanor Roosevelt, which actually applies to all people: "A woman is like a tea bag. You never know how strong it is until it's in hot water." Here's a similar analogy: People who are successful are like tea bags. When they get in hot water, they make tea. When life squeezes them, they don't become angry; they do something constructive with the pressure. They persevere under it and use it for their own benefit. People who have vision are stronger than the pressure life brings.

I have discovered that sometimes you don't get the scent from the rose until you crush it. In order to draw the fragrance of His glory from your life, God will allow you to be put under stress. We forget too easily that **character is formed by pressure.** The purpose of pressure is to get rid of what is not of God and to leave what is pure gold.

Are you willing to pay the price for your vision?

Perhaps you're in the fire right now. It's a good place to be. Go ahead and make tea. Surprise your enemies with the scent of God. Let them pressure you to release His glory. No matter what people may say about you, don't retaliate. Let them talk about you on your job. It doesn't matter what they think. You can smile, knowing that you will come through the situation. The Scriptures say it is not those who are swift, but those who endure to the end, who succeed. (See Matthew 24:13; Mark 13:13; James 5:11.)

Therefore, don't run—stay in the fight! **There is no stopping a person who understands that pressure is good for him because pressure is one of the keys to perseverance.**

Accept the Cost

Let me confess something to you: I wish I didn't have to be doing what I'm doing. I didn't say that I don't want to. I said I wish I didn't have to. That is not a negative statement, just a realistic one, because I know what the cost of my vision is going to be. In the next twenty or thirty years of my life, I know the cost is going to be high. That's why I thank God that, earlier in my life, I had the privilege of observing firsthand the cost to another visionary, who told me, "Myles, my son, get ready for the price." Because of that experience, I have been prepared to accept the cost.

At times, you will find it difficult to remain in your vision. I understand. It's tough for me to stay in mine. The demands that God is making on my ministry are high because the call

197

requires it. There's a price. Vision always demands a cost. Someone has to pay the price. Are you willing to do it? We need to be
like Paul, who was obedient to the vision God had given him to
do, even at great sacrifice.

Tested for Authenticity

Every true vision will be tested for authenticity. If your
vision is authentic, life is going to try it, just to make sure. Don't
be afraid when you make a declaration of what you're going to
do in life and difficulty follows; it comes to test your resolve.
All of us will encounter crises in life, but these crises don't have
to be setbacks. We should realize that a crisis can be a turning point at which our understanding of and commitment to
the vision is tested and matured. A crisis can lead us to greater
challenge and victory.

If a vision is stopped or terminated by trials or tests, then
perhaps it was not really a vision from God. Knowing this truth
can help you when you are considering whether or not to become
part of a corporate vision. Be careful not to become involved in
superficial enterprises. Check things out beforehand. Put the
vision to the test.

Ready to Face the Opposition

When God showed Abraham the land that his descendants
would inherit, He told him that everything as far as he could
see would be his. However, the land was full of Moabites, Hit-
tites, Caananites, and Amorites—the Israelites' future enemies!
Likewise, whenever God shows us a vision, it is full of "enemies" or opposition that we can't see at first. Instead, the vision
looks great. But the enemies are still there. For example, perhaps God has shown you a business He wants you to build. You
are excited about it, so you start to make plans. Yet, in the land
that God has shown you, there are a number of people who
are saying, "Just try to come and get it! You have to get past us
first!" Even though the promise is already yours, there are certain enemies you'll have to work through before you can see its

fulfillment. God doesn't show you the "ites" right away because He doesn't want to frighten you. He's building up your faith to prepare you for the time when you are ready to face the opposition and overcome it.

Therefore, if you are just now encountering some of the "enemies of the land," be encouraged that your faith is being strengthened and that God is not only enabling you to stand strong in the face of opposition to your vision, but also to overcome it—to His glory and praise.

Action Steps to Fulfilling Vision

- In what areas of your life/vision are you in need of perseverance?

- What have you given up on that you need to pick up again and continue on with?

- Ask God to develop faithfulness, steadfastness, and courage in you.

- Write down the saying, "Destiny demands diligence," on a piece of paper and put it where you can be reminded of it every day.

Chapter Principles

1. Obstacles will come against you and your vision. You must be persistent if you are going to achieve the vision God has given you.

2. Faithfulness means being true to what you have decided to accomplish and letting nothing stop you.

3. Steadfastness means to stand fast or stand steady in the face of resistance.

4. Courage is the ability to stand up in the face of fear.

5. Fear is a positive thing when it gives birth to courage.

6. Even though there will be times of stress, disappointment, and pressure, your vision *will* come to pass.

7. Every resistance to your vision comes to make you wiser, not weaker. Every opposition comes to strengthen you, not to stop you.

8. Destiny demands diligence.

9. Many people lose because they quit when life says no the first time, but persistent people win. They never take no for an answer when it comes to their visions.

10. There is not enough darkness in the world to extinguish the light God has put within you.

11. Perseverance means "to bear up under pressure."

12. Character is formed by pressure. The purpose of pressure is to get rid of what is not of God and to leave what is pure gold.

13. There is no stopping a person who understands that pressure is good for him because pressure is one of the keys to perseverance.

14. It is not those who are swift, but those who endure to the end, who succeed. (See Matthew 24:13; Mark 13:13; James 5:11.)

15. Vision always demands a cost.

16. Every true vision will be tested for authenticity.

Chapter Fourteen
Principle #11:
Be Patient in the Fulfillment of Vision

IMITATE THOSE WHO THROUGH FAITH AND PATIENCE INHERIT
WHAT HAS BEEN PROMISED.
—HEBREWS 6:12

Principle number eleven is that we must be patient in seeing the fulfillment of our visions. Again, it may take a while for your vision to come to fruition, but if you are willing to wait for it (which many people are not), it will come to pass. The writer of Hebrews tells us, *Do not throw away your confidence; it will be richly rewarded. You need to persevere ["have need of patience" KJV] so that when you have done the will of God, you will receive what he has promised* (Hebrews 10:35–36). People who have long patience will always win.

Patience Ensures the Eventual Success of the Plan

When some people make plans to carry out their visions, they try to force those plans into their own timetable or their own way of bringing them to pass. However, you cannot rush a vision. It is given by God, and He will carry it out in His own time. You may ask, "Then what is the reason for developing a plan in the first place?" Remember that the reason why you make plans is so you can have plans to modify, as necessary and appropriate, along the way—while still keeping to the overall vision. We are not all-knowing, as God is. We need to patiently rely on His guidance every step of the way. Remember that He promises to take us step-by-step, not leap-by-leap. Part of that step-by-step process is making some adjustments to the plan as the working out of His purposes becomes clearer to us.

Be willing to progress at the vision's pace.

As I wrote earlier, when we first receive our visions, we are not ready for them yet. The vision process takes us to the point at which we are ready for them to be fulfilled. If God showed us the entire path right away, we might balk at it. As we grow and mature along the path, however, we are able to follow God's leading and adjust our expectations and plans accordingly. We learn to follow the subtle leading of the Holy Spirit in our lives in which we *"hear a voice behind* [us]*, saying, 'This is the way; walk in it'"* (Isaiah 30:21).

Again, **you should always put deadlines on your goals, but you must also be willing to rearrange those deadlines;** be assured that the vision is coming at just the right time. God sent Jesus to be our Savior about four thousand years after the fall of humankind. Humanly speaking, that was a long time to wait. But He came just as predicted and at just the right time. The Bible says, *"But when the time had fully come, God sent his Son, born of a woman, born under law, to redeem those under law, that we might receive the full rights of sons"* (Galatians 4:4–5). Jesus came in the fullness of time, and so will your vision. That is why you need to be patient with your dream as you wait for it with anticipation. If someone asks you about it, say, "I'm just waiting for the next move." Some people might wonder if it will ever happen. You do not need to wonder, however, but simply to wait. It will all come to pass if you are willing to progress at the vision's pace.

If God has shown you that you will own a store, but right now, you are just working in one, then you can be happy and content, knowing that what you see with your eyes is not the vision you see in your heart; you can be certain that your current situation is only temporary. Or perhaps, right now, it is your job to make coffee for the boss. You're "enduring the shame" (see Hebrews 12:2) because you know you're going to be a general manager one day. Making coffee doesn't bother you, so you make the best coffee you possibly can. Perhaps people think you are just a secretary, but you know you're on your way to becoming a supervisor, so their opinion of you really doesn't matter. Vision makes you patient.

Patience Brings Peace in the Midst of Uncertainty

When you are patient in the fulfillment of your vision, you are able to be calm in the midst of uncertainty. For example, you can be at peace when everyone else is worrying about being laid off. No one can really "lay off" a child of God. All they can do is set you up for your next position that will further prepare you for the fulfillment of your vision. You can endure the cross when you have seen the joy of the end of your vision. (See Hebrews 12:2.)

When you don't have vision, you complain about the cross. You become frustrated about your position. You get angry about your salary. You worry about holding on to your job. You grumble. However, when you understand vision, you remember that **vision takes time and patience and often involves change.** To go to a new place, you have to think differently. As I wrote earlier, vision may constantly keep you unsettled, but it will also keep you fluid and mobile, ready to take the next step toward your vision. When you keep company with God, you have to keep moving, but you have the assurance that He is always with you along the path toward your vision's fulfillment.

Patience Overcomes Adversity

Patience is also the key to power over adversity and turmoil. If you threaten a man, and he just waits, your threat is going to wear off. The Bible says that a patient man is stronger than a mighty warrior: *"Better a patient man than a warrior, a man who controls his temper than one who takes a city"* (Proverbs 16:32).

When I first read that verse, I found it hard to believe that patience is more powerful than might. Then I came to understand the power of patience. A patient person makes others unsettled because they want that person to react to them, to become angry—but he never does. Nothing can make you more nervous than a waiting person. You try everything, and all he does is just wait. His waiting eventually unnerves and overcomes the opposition.

Therefore, when you have vision, no one can offend you. Do

Where there's hope, there's life.

your coworkers dislike you? That's all right. It's just temporary. Are they not speaking to you? That's okay. It's just temporary. Are they trying to hold you back? No problem. It's just temporary. Your job is not your life. It's merely a classroom to prepare you for your future.

Patience Wins the Race

As long as you can dream, there's hope. As long as there's hope, there's life. It's crucial that you and I maintain our dreams by patiently waiting for their fulfillment in the fullness of time. James 1:4 says, *"But let patience have its perfect work, that you may be perfect and complete, lacking nothing"* (NKJV). Others who have gone before us have had their faith tested, and it has produced patience in them (see verse 3) so that they were able to win the race. Let us do the same. Hebrews 12:1 says, *"Wherefore seeing we also are compassed about with so great a cloud of witnesses, let us lay aside every weight, and the sin which doth so easily beset us, and let us run with patience the race that is set before us"* (KJV). Amen.

Action Steps to Fulfilling Vision

- Have you been trying to force the timetable of the fulfillment of your vision? If so, what have you learned about patience in this chapter that will enable you to trust God to fulfill the vision in His timing?

• Encourage your spirit as you patiently wait for your vision to come to pass by committing these verses to memory this week:

> But let patience have its perfect work, that you may be perfect and complete, lacking nothing.   (James 1:4 NKJV)

> We do not want you to become lazy, but to imitate those who through faith and patience inherit what has been promised.   (Hebrews 6:12)

> You need to persevere so that when you have done the will of God, you will receive what he has promised.   (Hebrews 10:36)

Chapter Principles

1. We must be patient in seeing the fulfillment of our visions.

2. *"Do not throw away your confidence; it will be richly rewarded. You need to persevere ["have need of patience" KJV] so that when you have done the will of God, you will receive what he has promised"* (Hebrews 10:35–36).

3. People who have long patience will always win. Patience ensures the eventual success of your vision's plan.

4. We cannot try to force our visions into our own timetables. Vision is given by God, and He will carry it out in His own time.

5. Your vision will come to pass if you are willing to progress at the vision's pace.

6. When you are patient in the fulfillment of your vision, you are able to be calm in the midst of uncertainty.

7. Vision takes time and patience and often involves change.

8. Patience is the key to power over adversity and turmoil.

9. The testing of our faith produces patience, and patience perfects our spiritual character and leads to the fulfillment of our visions. (See James 1:4.)

10. *"Wherefore seeing we also are compassed about with so great a cloud of witnesses, let us lay aside every weight, and the sin which doth so easily beset us, and let us run with patience the race that is set before us"* (Hebrews 12:1 KJV).

Chapter Fifteen
Principle #12:
Stay Connected to the
Source of Vision

I AM THE VINE; YOU ARE THE BRANCHES....APART FROM ME YOU CAN
DO NOTHING.
—JOHN 15:5

Principle number twelve is that, if you are going to be successful in your vision, you must have a daily, dynamic personal prayer life with God. Why? Because you need continual communion and fellowship with the Source of vision.

Remember that you were born to consult God to find out His purpose for your life so that you can discover your vision. Yet, as the *"Alpha and the Omega, the Beginning and the End"* (Revelation 1:8 NKJV), God is not only the Author of your vision, but also your continuing Support as you progress toward its fulfillment. You will never achieve your vision without prayer because prayer is what keeps you connected to the Vision-Giver. Jesus said in John 15:5, *"I am the vine; you are the branches....Apart from me you can do nothing."* **If you stay in touch with God, you will always be nourished in both life and vision.**

Prayer Sustains Us in the Demands of Vision

Sometimes, in the pursuit of your vision, you will grow emotionally and spiritually weary if things don't seem to be working out for you. When you have been pressed, criticized, and opposed, you can become weak in faith. That is when you must stagger back to your prayer closet and say, "God, I want to give up," so that you can hear Him say to you, "What you began will be finished." Philippians 1:6 says, *"He who began a good work in you will carry it on to completion."* Prayer is the place where you can take all your burdens to God and say, "God, I *have* to make it," and He will say, "I'm with you. What are you afraid of?" *"The Lord is my light and my salvation—whom shall I fear? The Lord is the stronghold of my life—of whom shall I be afraid?"* (Psalm 27:1). God will bring you through your difficulties and give you the victory through prayer based on His Word.

Allow God to refresh you and rebuild your faith.

There are many days (and nights) when I stumble into my prayer room and say, "God, if You won't help me in this, I want You to take me home to You." Visions can be very demanding. It can be difficult running a business. It can be tough trying to start a new company. It can be hard trying to pursue a new aspect of your vision or doing something that no one else has ever done before. It can be stressful trying to go to school to earn a degree. Sometimes, you will feel, "Am I ever going to make it?" That's a good time to run to God. Prayer means getting away from the noise and confusion of life and saying, "God, I'm not going back out there." Yet if you will let Him encourage and refresh you, by the time you have finished praying, you will be saying, "I'm ready to go again!"

Prayer Encourages Us to Get Back in the Fight

Through our prayers, God also encourages us to get back out into the fight of faith. Isaiah 40:31 says, *"Those who hope in the Lord will renew their strength. They will soar on wings like eagles; they will run and not grow weary, they will walk and not be faint."* Yes, you will become tired, and sometimes you will want to quit. However, if you are willing to bear up in prayer and stand before God and say, "God, I'm hoping in you!" He will give you strength.

When you achieve your vision, and other people see you enjoying the victory, they will be proud of what you have accomplished. You'll have your belt on as the champion. Of course, they won't know about the rounds you lost, how you sometimes staggered as you made your way back into your corner to recuperate for the next round. A real fighter doesn't wear his medals on his chest. He wears them on his back. They are his scars. Only a few people will know what it took for you to achieve your vision. Yet you must be willing to take the scars if you want to wear the crown.

Allow God to strengthen you.

Believe me, every champion does not win every round, but if he perseveres, he wins the match. Since prayer is where you receive the ability to continue the fight, it is crucial for you to find times during the day when you can go to God and say things like, "God, I'm scared," so that He can reassure you that He is with you. He says, *"Surely I am with you always"* (Matthew 28:20). When you hear that, it is enough. You are be able to say, "Let's go back, Lord, and fight one more day." You can win, you can be victorious, if you are willing to take what you are afraid of to God in prayer.

Prayer Is the Essential Resource of Vision

Without prayer, you cannot get where you want to go. There will be times when all you'll have is prayer. You won't have any money, people, or resources—just prayer. Yet that is all you need. God will see you through.

When all the trouble and opposition came to Nehemiah, he said to God, *"Remember Tobiah and Sanballat, O my God, because of what they have done; remember also the prophetess Noadiah and the rest of the prophets who have been trying to intimidate me"* (Nehemiah 6:14). Nehemiah took all his troubles and enemies to God in prayer. He didn't write a letter of complaint to the editor of the newspaper. He didn't try to justify himself. He prayed, and God answered his prayer to deliver him. (See verses 15–16.)

God has invested Himself in your dream, and He will bring it to pass.

Likewise, **when people attack your dream, go to God. Don't try to explain and give an answer for everything because you can't explain anything to critics.** Their motives are already contaminated, and they'll use your words against you. Instead, stay connected to your Source for the renewal of your purpose, faith, and strength, and you will be able to persevere to victory. God is the One who planted your life's purpose within you in the beginning. He has invested Himself in your dream, and He will bring it to pass. *"If the LORD delights in a man's way, he makes his steps firm; though he stumble, he will not fall, for the LORD upholds him with his hand "* (Psalm 37:23–24).

Action Steps to Fulfilling Vision

- Establish a daily prayer time with God.
- In what ways are you relying on God for your life and vision? In what ways aren't you relying on Him? Commit to prayer the areas in which you aren't currently relying on Him. Be honest with Him about how you are feeling, and allow Him to strengthen, sustain, and encourage you through His presence and His Word.

Chapter Principles

1. To be successful in your vision, you must have a daily, dynamic prayer life with God.

2. God is not only the Author of your vision, but also your continuing Support as you progress toward its fulfillment.

3. You will never achieve your vision without prayer because prayer is what keeps you connected to the Vision-Giver.

4. If you stay in touch with God, you will always be nourished in both life and vision.

5. Prayer sustains us in the demands of vision. God will bring you through your difficulties and give you the victory through prayer based on His Word.

6. Prayer encourages us to get back in the fight of faith.

7. Since prayer is where we receive the ability to continue the fight, it is crucial for us to find times during the day when we can go before God.

8. Prayer is the essential resource of vision. When people attack your dream, go to God. Remain connected to your Source for the renewal of your purpose, faith, and strength, and you will be able to persevere to victory.

9. God is the One who planted your life's purpose within you in the beginning. He has invested Himself in your dream, and He will bring it to pass.

Part III

The Power of Vision

Chapter Sixteen

The Generational Nature
of Vision

YOU WERE BORN TO DO SOMETHING IN LIFE THAT LEAVES NUTRIENTS
FOR THE SEED OF THE NEXT GENERATION TO TAKE ROOT IN AND GROW.

Ecclesiastes 3:1 says, *"There is a time for everything, and a season for every activity under heaven."* Like the calendar year, our lives have four seasons, and those seasons must come to pass. The first season is birth and dependency. All of us go through this season in which we must rely totally on outside help, particularly our families, for survival. We need to be taught and trained in what is right and wrong and what is important in life.

The second season is one of independence, in which we capture what we were born to do. We no longer depend on other people to give us a vision for life or to help us survive. We focus in on our own goals. We depend primarily on God, yet we rely on the help of other people to provide the resources that will enable us to live out our dreams.

The third season is interdependence. In this stage, we have become so free in our visions that we can give our dreams to other people. We can now pass on our visions to the next generation.

The final season is death, where our lives become the nourishment for other people's dreams in the next generation. **If people can't receive life from the legacy you leave when you die, then you really didn't live effectively.** People should be able to flourish on the fruit of the vision you leave behind on earth.

Make your life on earth count— for yourself and others.

If it wasn't for their tombstones, we wouldn't know that some people were ever alive. What a tragedy. You should live so effectively that there won't be any need for a tombstone to mark your grave because your life will be in the hearts and memories of those who could never forget you or what you did. Truly great people don't need monuments because we will always remember them. It doesn't matter if we don't know where the graves of David or Joshua are. They lived so well that we can't forget them. If you live properly, history will not be able to ignore that you lived.

Vision gives us assignments that will impact the earth. We must be able to say we have changed the world in some way while we were here and that we have left a mark for those who will come after us. We were born to do something in life that leaves nutrients for the seeds of the next generation to take root in and grow. The fact is, we will soon be gone from this earth. Let's make the few years we have count! Let's discover and pursue the visions God has placed in our hearts.

Chapter Seventeen
How to Write Your Personal Vision Plan

GOD WILL DIRECT YOUR STEPS WHEN YOU MAKE A CONCRETE PLAN
TO MOVE TOWARD WHAT YOU DESIRE.

COMMIT TO THE LORD WHATEVER YOU DO, AND YOUR PLANS
WILL SUCCEED.
—PROVERBS 16:3

Most of us are trying to construct our lives without any real thought or planning. We are like a contractor who is trying to construct a building without a blueprint. As a result, our lives are out of balance and unreliable. We never fulfill the reason for our existence and end up unsatisfied and frustrated. The key to having a rewarding and productive life is developing a specific plan to fulfill your personal life vision.

Discovering and implementing your personal vision is a process of learning about yourself, growing in your relationship and knowledge of the Lord, and continually fine-tuning your understanding of the vision God has given you. Therefore, when you write your vision, realize that it won't be a finished product. You will keep refining it as God makes your purpose clearer as the months and years go by, and as you experience spiritual and personal growth. In fact, it would be a good idea

217

to review your personal vision on a regular basis. At least every six months to a year, set aside a block of time to pray and reevaluate where you are in relation to your vision. You will add to or take away certain elements of your plan as God refines your understanding of His purpose. Eventually, you will begin to see, "This is the real thing!" However, if you never write out a life blueprint, then God will have nothing to direct you in.

My prayer is that you will stop the construction of your life right where it is and go back and draw solid blueprints that will lead you where you want to go in life through the vision God has put in your heart. The following are guidelines for discovering and developing your personal vision plan. The last section of the book, "Taking Action: Action Steps to Bringing Your Vision into Reality," contains additional principles and guidelines for developing your vision plan, including a Personal Planning and Goal-Setting Program.

Step One: Eliminate Distractions

Sit down somewhere by yourself, away from any distractions and responsibilities, and allow yourself some uninterrupted time to think. Do this as often as you need to as you develop your plan.

Step Two: Find Your True Self

Until you know who you are, why God created you, and why you're here, life will simply be a confusing experiment. Answering the following questions will help give you clarity and confidence in regard to your personal identity.

- Who am I?
- Who am I in relation to God?
- Where do I come from as a person?
- How have I been created like my Source? (See Genesis 1:26–28.)
- Why am I here?

Write out your personal purpose statement. Ask yourself, What is my reason for existence as a human being and as an individual? (You may be able to answer this question only after you have completed the other steps. However, you may also want to write an answer now and then compare it with what you think after you have gone through the rest of the questions.)

Step Three: Find Your True Vision

Answer the following questions, and you'll be amazed at the way God will begin to open your mind to His purpose and vision for you. You'll begin to see things that you've never seen before. Put them down on paper, read them over, think about them, pray about them, and begin to formulate ideas of what you want out of life.

Ask yourself the following:

- What do I want to do with my life?
- What am I inspired to do?
- What would I want to do more than anything else, even if I was never paid for it?
- What do I love to do so much that I forget to eat or sleep?

Allow yourself to think freely. Don't put any limitations of time or money on your vision. Because many of us are influenced by others' opinions of us and by our own false expectations for ourselves, it may take you a little time to discover what you really want. Persevere through the process and dig down deep to find your true desires. Below are activities to help you do this.

Activities:

Write your own legacy.

- What you would like your eulogy to say about you? What would you like to be known for? What would you want others (for example, family members, colleagues, teachers, employers, neighbors) to say about you?

- Family: What kind of husband, wife, son, or daughter do you want to be remembered as?
- Society: What kind of impact would you like to leave on your community?
- World: In what way would you like the world to be different because you were here?

Write out your personal mission statement.

Your mission statement is a general statement of what you want to have accomplished when your life is over. Ask yourself where you want to be one, five, ten, twenty, thirty years from now. Jot down your ideas and continue to think and pray about them.

Summarize your vision for your life in just one sentence.

This is a specific statement of what you want to do in life. It should be what motivates you and keeps you going toward your dream.

Step Four: Discover Your True Motivation

A vision from God is never selfish. It will always help or uplift others in some way. It is designed to make the lives of humankind better and to improve society. It inspires and builds up others.

Ask yourself the following:

- How does my vision help others?
- What is the motivation for my vision?
- Why do I want to do what I want to do?
- Can I accomplish my vision and still have integrity?

Step Five: Identify Your Principles

Your principles are your philosophy of life. In other words, they are how you intend to conduct yourself during your life. You must clarify what you will and won't do. These principles are your guides for living, doing business, relating to other people, and relating to life. You must settle them in your heart and mind so that you will have standards to live by.

The Ten Commandments are great principles and a good starting point for developing your own principles. For example, you could write, "On my way to my vision, I will not steal, lie, or bear false witness. I won't worship any god but God the Father. I will not commit adultery. I will not covet," and so on.

- Write out your life principles.

Step Six: Choose Your Goals and Objectives

Goals are the steps necessary to fulfill your vision. What practical things do you need to do to accomplish your dream? Goals are clear markers that will take you where you need to go.

- Write out your goals.

Objectives are the detailed steps of your goals. They determine when you want things to happen. You must clearly delineate what you need to do and when you need to do it in order to get to where you want to go. For example, if you want to open a mechanics shop, and one of your goals is to go to school to learn mechanics, some of your objectives will be to choose a school, fill out an application, and start classes. Objectives should include specific timetables.

- Write out your objectives.

Step Seven: Identify Your Resources

You now need to identify all the resources you will need to accomplish your vision.

Identify your human needs.

What help do you need from others to fulfill your vision? What kind of personal associations do you need to have—and not have?

Identify your resource needs.

What kinds of resources do you need to fulfill your vision? Don't worry about how large they may seem. Write them down.

Write down your strengths.

Who are you? What are your gifts? What do you know you are good at? Write down your answers, and then make plans to refine your strengths. For example, if your vision requires that you have to speak before large groups of people, you have to start stepping out and doing it. You're probably going to be scared at first, yet God will give you opportunities to speak at different stages so you can develop your gift. You don't even know what you can do until you have to. Some amazing gifts come out of people when they are under pressure.

Write down your weaknesses.

What does your vision need that you aren't good at? Don't be ashamed of your weaknesses, because everyone has something they are not good at. You don't have the monopoly on that. However, you must identify them because God will supply other people to do what you cannot do toward your vision. You need other people in your life because your vision cannot be fulfilled by you alone.

Step Eight: Commit to Your Vision

You will never fulfill your vision if you are not committed to it. You will need to make a specific decision that you are going to follow through with what you want to do, acknowledging that God may refine your plans as He leads you through the process. Also, commit your vision to God on a regular basis. Proverbs 16:3 says, *"Commit to the LORD whatever you do, and your plans will succeed."*

- Commit to your vision.
- Commit your vision to God.

Taking Action

ACTION STEPS TO BRINGING YOUR VISION INTO REALITY

The Principles and Process of Vision

- Sight is a function of the eyes, but vision is a function of the heart. "Eyes that look are common, but eyes that see are rare." Without vision, sight has no hope.

- Sight is the ability to see things as they are; vision is the capacity to see things as they could be.

- *"Faith is the substance of things hoped for, the evidence of things not seen* [with the natural eye]" (Hebrews 11:1 NKJV). Faith is seeing the future in the present. Faith is vision.

The Principles of Vision

1. Vision is the product of purpose.
2. Vision is the source of true leadership.
3. Vision is documented purpose.
4. Vision is detailed, customized, distinctive, unique, and reasonable.

5. Vision never maintains the status quo.
6. Vision always demands change.
7. Vision is future-focused.
8. Vision creates self-discipline.
9. Vision is a result of godly inspiration.
10. Vision is not the mission.
11. Vision is generational.
12. Vision is manifested in phases.
13. Vision is always given to individuals.
14. Vision is greater than the visionary.
15. Vision is more powerful than death.
16. Vision empowers people to action.

The Process of Vision

1. Vision must be captured.
2. Vision must be simplified.
3. Vision must be documented.
4. Vision must be communicated.
5. Vision must be shared ownership.
6. Vision must be both personal and corporate.
7. Vision must produce a plan.
8. Vision must be constantly revised.
9. Vision must be evaluated.
10. Vision must create priorities.

How to Write a Mission Statement

A mission is a general statement of purpose that declares the overall idea of what you want to accomplish. It is philosophical and abstract rather than practical and concrete.

A written mission statement defines the purpose and justification for your existence (personal and corporate). To write your personal mission statement, ask yourself the following questions:

1. What represents the deepest and best within me?

2. What would fulfill my gifts and express my capacity to contribute to humanity?

3. What integrates all my physical, mental, social, and spiritual needs?

4. What creates and reflects my principle-based values?

5. What would fulfill all my roles in life—family, professional, community, and generational?

How to Write Your Personal Vision

True vision is the product of a clear sense of purpose and deep inspiration. The following questions will help you to identify and refine your personal vision.

1. What is my deepest desire?

2. What do I want to leave to this generation as a contribution?

3. What is the idea that never leaves me?

4. What do I constantly imagine about my future?

5. What do I feel truly passionate about?

6. What one thing would I do if I knew I could not fail?

7. What do I see my future looking like?

8. What is the most important thing I wish I could do in my life?

9. What are my constant, reoccurring dreams?

10. What would bring me the greatest fulfillment?

Keys to Fulfilling Your Vision

• IDENTIFY •

• CLARIFY •

• REFINE •

• DOCUMENT •

• ARTICULATE •

• COMMUNICATE •

• DEMONSTRATE •

• REEVALUATE •

• REVISE •

• REPEAT •

• *VISION SIMPLIFIES LIFE* •

Personal Plan Program: A Systematic Strategy

To fulfill the plans for your life, it is necessary to discipline yourself and submit to wise counsel, as it is written: *"Plans fail for lack of counsel, but with many advisers they succeed"* (Prov. 15:22).

The following questions must be answered and fulfilled for the success of your plans:

1. What do I want to accomplish?
2. Who do I need?
3. Where can I go for information?
4. What do I need to read?
5. Who should I associate with?
6. How long should it take?
7. How much will it cost?
8. What courses should I take?
9. Where can I get experience?
10. What do I have?

Seven Principles of Vision (from Habakkuk 2:1-4)

1. The principle of documentation (write the vision)
2. The principle of simplification (make it plain)
3. The principle of shared vision (give it to the heralds)
4. The principle of participation (let them run with it)
5. The principle of timing (an appointed time)
6. The principle of patience (wait for it)
7. The principle of faith (it will certainly come)

Personal Planning and Goal-Setting Program

Year:_____

Name:_____

     By God's grace, I commit to accomplishing the following goals this year:

Personal Spiritual Goals

1. _____
2. _____
3. _____

Personal Family Goals

1. _____
2. _____
3. _____

Personal Health Goals

1. _____
2. _____
3. _____

Personal Academic Goals

1. _____
2. _____
3. _____

Personal Career Goals

1. _____
2. _____
3. _____

Personal Relationship Goals

1. _____
2. _____
3. _____

Personal Financial Goals

1. _____
2. _____
3. _____

Personal Investment Goals

1. _____
2. _____
3. _____

(See sample goals on page 230.)

I PRESS ON TOWARD THE GOAL TO WIN THE PRIZE FOR WHICH GOD
HAS CALLED ME HEAVENWARD IN CHRIST JESUS.
—PHILIPPIANS 4:13

Sample Goals:

- read seven books on spiritual subjects
- increase communication with family
- lose weight
- get a physical checkup
- earn a master's degree
- take continuing education courses
- meet five new friends
- open a savings account
- reduce or eliminate all financial debt
- purchase real estate

A Word to Third-World Nations

The ability to dream is the greatest power on earth. The ability to see your hope is the greatest motivator of humanity. The ability to imagine and incubate a vision is inherent in the human spirit and manifests itself in the daydreams of every child. This gift of imagination and the capacity to cultivate aspirations is the impartation of the Spirit of the Creator of all things. It provides mankind with the power to hope beyond the present—an ability that has motivated the human race throughout the ages to believe in an unseen future. Without hope, life has no positive future, and disillusionment becomes a way of life. The ability to dream is the greatest power on earth because it is the essence of true faith.

Life was designed to be lived intentionally and on purpose, but most of the people of the world exist under circumstances beyond their control. They live by duress rather than destiny. It is said that the poorest person in the world is the person without a dream. When the dream dies, the human spirit dies. The greatest tragedy in life is not death, but life without a purpose. Purpose is the source of meaning in life and serves as the womb for the conception of dreams and visions. Therefore, the greatest injustice that can be imposed on the human spirit is the termination of its ability to dream and have a vision. Remember the principle of King Solomon: *"Where there is no vision, the people perish"* (Prov. 29:18 KJV). The capacity to dream is the ability to keep living. In essence, to have a purpose is to discover hope, to hope is to dream, to dream is to cultivate a vision, to possess a vision is to have faith, and to have faith is to have a reason to live. There is no greater robbery than to steal vision from a person or a people, for to destroy vision is to destroy life.

Of the over six billion people on planet earth today, I estimate that about four billion are struggling with the reality of a visionless, dreamless life. For most, history has robbed them of the capacity to dream and to live with hope for a better future. Millions live in nations, societies, and communities that are products of years of oppression and suppression. Hundreds of years of colonialism, dictatorships, and slavery have rendered them visually dull—motivated only by a spirit to survive. They live for immediate gratification and plan only for each day. Many have no sense of purpose, hope, vision, or a future, and they struggle daily to make life work.

These people represent the largest percentage of the human population and have been defined as Third-World developing nations. Historically speaking, Third-World people are defined as those who either did not or were not allowed to participate in or benefit from the industrial revolution. Many were victims of slavery, indentured servitude, and subjection to imperialist powers. Today, despite the proliferation of achievement of national independence by many of these peoples, most are still struggling with the reality of economic, technological, political, and social colonialism.

The impact of oppression on these people has been devastating. They have experienced the loss of self-worth, self-esteem, self-concept, and a sense of dignity. However, the greatest tragedy of oppression was the destruction of the capacity to dream and have vision. The result is that many of these nations, even after many years of national independence, are still locked in a time warp of self-defeating behavior.

"Where there is no vision, the people perish" could describe many of the developing Third-World nations, where successive governments are challenged by a lack of national pride, a poor

work ethic, a culture of corruption, and their citizenry's loss of hope. Many of the political, civic, and religious leaders of these nations also lack the perspective of a long-term vision approach to governing and leadership. For most of these leaders, survival, suspicion, protectionism, and self-preservation are their primary motivators. A restoration of the visionary spirit and the capacity to dream is imperative.

A lack of visionary leaders has contributed to the state of many of these developing nations in Central America, Africa, the Caribbean, the Far East, and Asia. It is my hope that this new century will produce a new breed of leaders who are motivated by a sense of purpose and will exercise visionary leadership that inspires confidence and trust among the people. We need leaders to promote national visions that can birth the creative capacity of personal visions.

The wealth and natural resources in these developing nations are tremendous and, if properly managed, could eradicate the plight of poverty with which many of these countries are now commonly identified. The abuse, mismanagement, rape, and hoarding of this wealth have rendered many millions of people helpless, depressed, destitute, disillusioned, and devastated. The answer to this dilemma is not more foreign aid, United Nations handouts, or IMF debt-cancellation programs, but the conception of noble visions. We need the emergence of leadership that can see beyond their personal pockets and capture a God-inspired vision of the nation that incorporates the aspirations of the people and their right to pursue their personal dreams and visions. I believe the key is visionary leadership.

May the principles in this book be a source of igniting the passion of purpose in the hearts of this very special and unique group of people. May you be inspired to discover, pursue, and fulfill the visions in your hearts and maximize the potential trapped within you, potential that was buried in the historical grave of low self-esteem and self-doubt. May you dream dreams that inspire your children to dream and have visions of a better world. May your visions become reality and impact those who are not yet born. May the Third World live up to its destiny and set an example for all the world to see. May you see farther than your eyes can look.

About the Author

D r. Myles Munroe (1954–2014) was an international motivational speaker, best-selling author, educator, leadership mentor, and consultant for government and business. Traveling extensively throughout the world, Dr. Munroe addressed critical issues affecting the full range of human, social, and spiritual development. The central theme of his message is the maximization of individual potential, including the transformation of followers into leaders and leaders into agents of change.

Dr. Munroe was founder and president of Bahamas Faith Ministries International (BFMI), a multidimensional organization headquartered in Nassau, Bahamas. He was chief executive officer and chairman of the board of the International Third World Leaders Association and president of the International Leadership Training Institute.

Dr. Munroe was also the founder and executive producer of a number of radio and television programs aired worldwide. In addition, he was a frequent guest on other television and radio programs and international networks and was a contributing writer for various Bible editions, journals, magazines, and newsletters, such as *The Believer's Topical Bible, The African Cultural Heritage Topical Bible, Charisma Life Christian Magazine*, and *Ministries Today*. He was a popular author of more than forty books, including *The Power of Character in Leadership, The Purpose and Power of Authority, The Principles and Benefits of Change, Becoming a Leader, The Purpose and Power of the Holy Spirit, The Spirit of Leadership, The Principles and Power of Vision, Understanding the Purpose and Power of Prayer, Understanding the Purpose and Power of Women*, and *Understanding the Purpose and Power of Men*.

Dr. Munroe has changed the lives of multitudes around the world with a powerful message that inspires, motivates, challenges, and empowers people to discover personal purpose, develop true potential, and manifest their unique leadership abilities. For over thirty years, he trained tens of thousands of leaders in business, industry, education, government, and religion. He personally addressed over 500,000 people each year on personal and professional development. His appeal and message transcend age, race, culture, creed, and economic background.

Dr. Munroe earned B.A. and M.A. degrees from Oral Roberts University and the University of Tulsa, and was awarded a number of honorary doctoral degrees. He also served as an adjunct professor of the Graduate School of Theology at Oral Roberts University.

The parents of two adult children, Charisa and Chairo (Myles Jr.), Dr. Munroe and his wife, Ruth, traveled as a team and were involved in teaching seminars together. Both were leaders who ministered with sensitive hearts and international vision. In November 2014, they were tragically killed in an airplane crash en route to an annual leadership conference sponsored by Bahamas Faith Ministries International. A statement from Dr. Munroe in his book *The Power of Character in Leadership* summarizes his own legacy: "Remember that character ensures the longevity of leadership, and men and women of principle will leave important legacies and be remembered by future generations."